Sixty to Zero

Sixty to Zero

An Inside Look at the Collapse of General Motors—and the Detroit Auto Industry

ALEX TAYLOR III

Foreword by
Mike Jackson

Yale

UNIVERSITY PRESS

New Haven & London

Yale University Press books may be purchased in quantity for educational, business,
or promotional use. For information, please e-mail sales.press@yale.edu (U.S. office)
or sales@yaleup.co.uk (U.K. office).

Designed by James J. Johnson and set in Electra type by Integrated Publishing Solutions.
Printed in the United States of America.

The Library of Congress has cataloged the hardcover edition as follows:
Taylor, Alex, 1945–
    Sixty to zero : an inside look at the collapse of General Motors—and the Detroit auto
industry / Alex Taylor III ; foreword by Mike Jackson.
        p. cm.
    Includes index.
    ISBN 978-0-300-15868-7 (clothbound : alk. paper)   1. General Motors Corpora-
tion—Management.   2. Automobile industry and trade—Michigan—Detroit—
History   3. Bankruptcy—Michigan—Detroit—History.   I. Title.
    HD9710.U54G47574 2010
    338.7'62920973—dc22   2009052163

ISBN 978-0-300-17151-8 (pbk.)

A catalogue record for this book is available from the British Library.

10 9 8 7 6 5 4 3 2 1

To Maddie, Alexander, and, especially, Mary

Contents

Contents

Foreword

Few brands ever become so successful that they transcend the products and services they stand for and actually come to represent the countries and cultures from which they emerge. Coca-Cola is one—during the Second World War, GIs brought Coke with them to some of the remotest corners of the earth, and in the course of a few years, that hourglass-shaped bottle became a proxy for American power worldwide. McDonald's is another, introducing American middle-class sensibilities regarding food, convenience, and service to countries on six continents.

General Motors is a third. During the postwar boom, as domestic manufacturing reached its zenith, the company did more than simply mirror the American way of life—it helped to shape it, and for a time, the story of GM's rise was the story of America's ascendency.

In corporate structure, GM served as a model of efficiency and organization that hundreds of other businesses adopted, literally influencing the way millions of us made our livings. In ambition, GM's drive to diversify and dominate the industrial landscape was something that came straight from the days of the oil barons and that continues to this day in the form of multinational corporations.

In engineering and technology, GM produced machines that are as distinctive and evocative as any song or headline or fashion of the era. In personnel, GM's workforce was drawn from the patchwork of nationalities and ethnicities that called the Midwest home, people with names like Chromecki and Abbondanza and Dvorak and Williams.

In other words, GM helped produce postwar America as surely as America helped produce GM. No wonder, then, that GM president Charles Wilson famously said that "for years I thought what was good for our country was good for General Motors, and vice versa."

So what happened? How did a company that literally helped invent the most dominant, prosperous nation in the world fall so far and so fast?

That is the story Alex Taylor presents here, and it's a compelling one. It tells of how some of the sharpest, most inventive and resourceful people you could ever meet became victims of their own success, how hubris can take hold and destroy a company from the inside, and how circumstances can confound even the most surefire strategy at every opportunity. But more than that, it offers a glimpse at a company ready for rebirth — perhaps not as the power it once was, but as a chastened, humbled organization with the opportunity to reach for at least some of that past glory.

There are plenty of insights here for businesspeople today, regardless of the industry they serve. The lessons Taylor discusses have less to do with the automotive world than they do with the nature of organizations and the individuals who compose them. As the author shows, GM suffered the inevitable fate of any company that becomes so large and so dominant that it begins to believe its own infallibility. He catalogs in vivid detail the inevitable results of a system that required processes to be maintained at the expense of results. And he shows us the natural consequences of an environment where the fear of failure became greater than the promise of innovation.

As recently as a decade ago, it would have been almost inconceivable to imagine a world without General Motors. Nowadays, it's almost inconceivable to remember a time when GM was the apex of American industry. If there's anything that all of us can take from this story, it's that economic circumstances and human frailties can and will join together to conspire against us—especially when they seem most unlikely.

It's happened before. Few consumers now under 50 [ok? I'm 49, and I know about them only from my dad] remember Burma Shave or Ipana. Pan Am is only a memory for most of us, and Montgomery Ward is almost entirely forgotten. Yet each of these was once the General Motors of its industry—or close to it. How do we, as businesspeople, recognize and address decline before it takes on an uncontrollable life of its own?

Mathematicians have a concept they call regression to the mean: the idea that moments of peak performance tend to be followed by a return to a more normal operation. But where other companies simply pull back from their highs to produce longer runs of modest results, GM's decline was so steep and so fast that even simple stability would have been hailed as a success. Instead, the company rushed irresistibly towardsa catastrophic bottom, hurried along by a combination of circumstance and misjudgment that makes for high drama—and a compelling cautionary tale.

These are challenging problems to contend with, and they resonate across the broader economy. It's to our great benefit—and the benefit of those inside GM today—that Taylor so clearly and painstakingly illuminates the troubles as they occurred. Many of them would be considered minor on their own, but together, they took on a cumulative power that proved to be daunting. That was particularly so when coupled with more significant competitive, economic, legislative, and geopolitical concerns.

For a time, in fact, GM would have felt to those on the inside like a company deliberately under siege. Forces were amassed around the walls with destructive intent, while inside leadership was desperate to come up with a solution—any solution—to keep the invaders at bay. And like many classical sieges, it wasn't sheer force that brought down the walls but weaknesses from inside that ultimately created an environment where breach was inevitable.

I have a very personal stake in understanding the errors that led to GM's decline. As chairman and CEO of AutoNation—the country's largest automotive retailer—the mistakes GM has made have direct and specific parallels to the business that I operate. But that doesn't make its story any less relevant to other executives and managers and students of the modern corporation. In the decline of GM, we see the devastating results of individual misjudgments and misfortune, but also errors that arise from institutional problems and from issues related to the structure of the national and global economy.

It's a difficult lesson for many of us to learn today—it requires that we recognize just how tenuous success truly is and just how difficult it can be to sustain performance for an extended time. But for those of us who believe that our current financial crises are things to be overcome rather than harbingers of more challenging times ahead, for those of us who believe that America's best years are in the future rather than in the past, these are essential lessons for us to learn. Pay close attention to the story of General Motors, and we can make it something to remember rather than something to relive. The new GM is on the verge of being a Great Company again, and this brand icon will shine once more.

Mike Jackson, chairman and CEO, AutoNation

Acknowledgments

I wish to thank the editors of Time Inc. for permission to use copy-righted material from *Fortune* and *Time* magazines for historical research and to document my reporting on the auto industry.

Introduction

Because of its size and history, its products, and its advertising, General Motors, along with brands like Chevrolet and Cadillac, is a name instantly recognizable to people everywhere. Before their eyes, and mine, this great company—hailed as a monument to superior corporate management, technological achievement, and product excellence—spiraled downward for forty years before it crumbled into bankruptcy in 2009 and had to be rescued by the federal government. For years, GM was the largest automaker in the world and utterly dominated the American market. Now it is struggling to justify the investment of fifty billion dollars in taxpayer money to keep it alive.

No crimes were committed in GM's fall. There were no great scandals involving phony accounting, exploding derivatives, or elaborate Ponzi schemes. The seeds of its decline were planted long ago and for years covered up by its huge profitability, its dominant market share, and the ineptness of its domestic competitors. GM's collapse was caused, pure and simple, by bad management combined with ego and conceit. Successful for so long, GM executives couldn't conceive of a world in which the "GM way" wouldn't allow them to prosper indefinitely.

In many ways, the story of GM is a tragic one. The company fell because diligent, well-meaning individuals with traditional American values of thrift and hard work couldn't do things well enough despite years of trying to keep the company competitive and safeguard it from an economic downturn. In retrospect, it is shocking. In my more than thirty years of covering the auto industry, the vast majority of GM'ers I have met have been smart, sincere, dutiful, and diligent. But in working for the largest company in the world, they became self-referential, inwardly-focused, and wedded to the status quo—traits that persisted even when GM was on the brink of collapse. They preferred stability over change, continuity over disorder, and GM's way over anybody else's. Those personality defects turned out to be fatal.

GM's decline has been a uniquely public spectacle. No other company that I can think of has fallen so far for so long with so many people watching. The names of its executives are well known, as are their mistakes: inattention, bad judgment, and unwillingness to take risks. Their failure caused hundreds of thousands of white- and blue-collar workers to lose their jobs and millions of shareholders to see their investments completely wiped out. It remains an open question whether GM's latest CEO, Fritz Henderson, can do what his predecessors stretching back to the 1970s failed to do and discard enough of GM's bad old ways to allow the slimmed-down, postbankruptcy GM to survive.

In other ways, the story of GM is a tale of accumulating irrelevance. Competition tightened as new market entrants arrived, technology took big strides, customer preferences changed, and GM couldn't keep up. Some GM CEOs—Fred Donner, Dick Gerstenberg, Thomas Murphy—couldn't see what was happening. Others—Roger Smith, Jack Smith, Rick Wagoner—understood all too well that GM was sick but moved either too slowly or too ineffectively to find a cure. At the end, GM was no longer a national force. It had become a red-state company; Buicks and Pontiacs were still popular in the Midwest and South but seldom seen in California or New York City.

GM had been so caught up in its insular culture that it missed what was going on in the wider world. Authors Robert Monks and Nell Minow diagnosed it succinctly in their book *Corporate Governance* (2008): "GM was the premier car company in the world for so long that it failed to see the need for change. The company was so used to being leader that it couldn't contemplate following others. It was this mindset, this overwhelming belief that it was GM's divine right to be the most successful automobile company on earth, that condemned the company to two decades of disaster. When GM did finally see the need to adapt, it did with wild ineptitude, spending tens of billions in the 1980s for little reward. . . . GM. . . became living proof of the old boxing maxim: the bigger they are, the harder they fall."

The story of Rick Wagoner, who resigned in 2009, is especially tragic because he spent a decade trying to change GM first as president and then as CEO. He thought he knew what was wrong, and he believed he had enough time and money to correct it. "We're playing our own game," Wagoner used to say, "taking advantage of our own unique heritage and strengths." But time ran out on him. Wagoner was effectively fired by an Obama administration bureaucrat because GM's game wasn't good enough—and Wagoner either didn't realize it or couldn't do enough about it.

Back in 2004, when it was still flush, GM invited automotive journalists to the south of France for a three-day "global product seminar." The idea was that writers like me would drive new cars, consume loads of free food and wine, pal around with executives, and develop favorable opinions about the company. GM did its job. The accommodations at individual villas at the Four Seasons resort were five-star, the food was spectacular, and the weather was perfectly accommodating. We dined outdoors every day, and so many executives were available for so long that I ran out of questions to ask them. That is called journalistic nirvana.

On the first morning, the writers were supposed to team up with GM executives to drive to a nearby racetrack, the Paul Ricard circuit near Marseille, for lunch. Still a little jet-lagged, I arranged to drive with Wagoner, my favorite GM executive, in a yellow Corvette. I liked Wagoner because he was smart, personable, and thoughtful and because he was important. I've spent more hours with Wagoner than with all his predecessors combined, and I've never failed to be impressed by his depth and scope.

I had first met Rick Wagoner back in the late 1980s in Switzerland, where I had landed on an around-the-world reporting trip to see how GM Europe was faring. Wagoner and his then-boss, future GM chairman and CEO Jack Smith, met me one Saturday morning for an hour-long interview. Characteristically, Wagoner remembered the meeting, but I hadn't. Early on, Wagoner could be testy when confronted with writers like me who sometimes came bearing bad news. He once greeted me at a Detroit auto show with the sarcastic salutation "Here comes Mr. Sunshine," and he accused me during an interview of being "thickheaded." But under the tutelage of public relations guru Steve Harris, whom

Wagoner recruited from Chrysler, Wagoner had become more accommodating with reporters and generated an enormous amount of goodwill for himself and GM with his remodeled approach. If dealing with the media wasn't the favorite part of his work, he did a good job of hiding it.

I am not much of a sports car driver, but the Corvette was the only car available, and the fact that it had only two seats meant that Wagoner would be alone and our conversation wouldn't be interrupted by public relations people. My job was mostly to navigate while Wagoner drove, and I used the time to pepper him with questions. What an opportunity! I wanted to learn everything about life at the top of GM: the CEO's secret, special sources of information, his opinion about President George W. Bush, whom he had recently met; his views on competitors and industry trends. Since we were speaking off the record, Wagoner was responsive and candid. As for my route directions, he mostly ignored them and followed the car in front of us, also filled with journalists, which was headed in the same direction.

After two hours of driving, we discovered we had made a serious mistake: we missed the racetrack and wound up back at the hotel. It turned out I had been navigating from the wrong map, and the car in front of us, driven by Chinese journalists, was just as lost as we were. Lunch would be delayed while the CEO and I made our way to the track by way of a shortcut, meaning that I had effectively kidnapped the chairman of GM for three hours. Sure, we had been tailed the whole time by Wagoner's security detail in a separate car, but it remained behind us at a respectful distance and never stopped to ask us where we were going. That wasn't all. When the embarrassment and tension of it all attacked my blad-

der, I was forced to ask the head of this mighty industrial corporation for an impromptu roadside pit stop. Wagoner made the ar-
rangements with the security detail and added helpful suggestions
about how to avoid such emergencies in the future.

I learned two things from this episode. First, never underesti-
mate the ability of a know-it-all journalist to get it wrong or to fold
up like a cheap suitcase when the pressure is on. And second, at
some point good manners and civility become a liability rather
than an asset when running a giant company or getting lost. Those
are traits Wagoner shared with most other top GM managers.
Around Detroit, Ford executives were known as scrappers skilled at
bare-knuckle office politics. The joke was that they looked as if
they had all gotten their job in a back alley. The head guys at
Chrysler—Lee Iacocca, Bob Lutz (before he moved to GM), chief
engineer François Castaing—trafficked in bravado and charisma.
At GM, it was the nice guys who usually finished first, gentlemen
like Wagoner: the adult equivalent of Eagle Scouts. Too nice, as it
turned out. Those personality traits didn't serve the company well.

Quite often over the past three decades of automotive journalism, friends and readers have asked me whether I get tired of covering the car business. I've asked myself the same question and
have now and then gone off to write about other companies and
other industries: aerospace, consumer products, industrial equipment. But either by events or by force of habit, I keep getting
dragged back to autos. The news flow, which reached a peak in
2009 with the bankruptcy of both Chrysler and GM, is always
heavy. There are new models to review, monthly sales to report,
quarterly earnings to analyze. Companies rise and companies
fall, and each turning point is an opportunity for a story in *Fortune,*

where I worked for twenty-four years. Then there are sagas of larger scale and scope: the march of technology or the rise of overseas markets and the emergence of new international players. All merit coverage and space when the subject is cars, because no other industry has anything approaching its economic heft or visibility. Everyone owns a car or wants to own one or has an opinion about one. Unlike any other consumer product I can think of, cars are all around us, and most of us can tell one model and brand from another with a glance, and we know what our neighbor drives. That isn't true of mobile phones, running shoes, or soft drinks.

I've also found the industry personally rewarding to write about because of the opportunity it provides to build relationships. Despite its global scope, the auto world is surprisingly close-knit. Participants share a common passion: they got into the business because they love cars, and few voluntarily leave. Retirement before the age of sixty-five is rare—the pull is too strong, the action too good. I have been writing about some industry figures for more than twenty years. That's not possible in other businesses.

To abuse Hemingway, covering autos is like a movable journalistic feast. You travel around the world to conferences, shows, and product launches. On press days at the important international auto shows, executives from two dozen companies will be speaking with the same group of fifty to a hundred journalists they have been encountering at various venues all year. Similar conversations will have been held at shows in Paris and New York, and the same people will be talking with one another again at Detroit and Tokyo and Frankfurt.

Covering GM has always commanded a large chunk of my time. It is big, until recently the largest auto company in the world.

And it has been in the process of remaking itself for nearly as long as I have been a journalist, providing plentiful opportunities for coverage. GM's size makes reporting about it a challenging journalistic enterprise. Understanding it requires industry, enterprise, and guile. One of the key attributes is a good memory, being able to compare past promises to current achievements. Another is a thick Rolodex of sources, especially of former GM employees who have gone on to become analysts or consultants or to work for competitors. Covering GM also requires a large travel budget. I've visited GM operations in Germany, Japan, China, Chile, and Brazil, as well as the United States, all on the *Fortune* expense account.

General Motors wasn't the only U.S. automaker to face defining moments in 2009. Chrysler, once the most nimble and innovative company in Detroit, couldn't cope with the Great Recession either. Chrysler had been living by its wits since 1978, when Lee Iacocca arrived just in time to save it from bankruptcy. But the automaker was done in by feckless owners, a chronic shortage of capital, and the vicissitudes of the market. In a world of automotive overcapacity—too many plants, too many models, too many dealers—Chrysler's reasons for being, notably its trucks and minivans, were no longer sufficient. In 2009, Italy's Fiat stepped in to pick up what pieces remained of this once-vibrant company.

The story of Chrysler is a bipolar tale: moments of brilliance interwoven with spells of indifference and inattention. Like GM, Chrysler long ago understood its shortcomings but often was caught up in the moment and never fully got around to addressing them. Its product quality never rose above substandard, it remained dependent on hit products and light trucks, and it continued to focus on North America to the exclusion of the rest of the world. Those problems festered for thirty years and eventually became malignant.

Ford Motor has been on a similar roller-coaster ride, underwritten by the success of its F-series pickup, the most popular vehicle in America. With the Ford family behind the wheel, life at America's oldest automaker has been full of surprises, as executives fell in and out of favor with the royal family. Ford has seen nearly as many abrupt departures of chief executive officers in the past thirty years as GM and Chrysler combined. Some have gone quietly, some noisily.

In 2006, Ford had the good fortune to hire an experienced industrial manager, Boeing's Alan Mulally, to guide the company through a restructuring, and the good sense to borrow a wad of money before the downturn gained momentum. Ford's signal moment of 2009 was its decision not to follow GM and Chrysler to the government trough for federal loans and to try to survive without a Washington bailout. But these are early days for this latest chapter in Ford's 106-year-history, and the full measure of Mulally's success will not be known for several years.

During my time at *Fortune*, automobiles have been the largest advertising category. At some publications, that would be an invitation for editorial interference—negative stories don't provide a positive environment in which to promote new models with four-color ads—but despite my sometimes critical coverage, I never heard a word from anyone who was responsible for selling ads or otherwise worried about the bottom line. The separation between church (editorial) and state (the business side of the magazine) remained intact.

Except once. In 1990, GM was struggling during the last year of Roger Smith's disastrous tenure as CEO, and I had prepared a harsher-than-usual article on the company. Rather than relying on my memory to tell what happened next, let me refer to an account published in the "Intelligencer" section of *New York* magazine in its April 2, 1990, issue. My boss, Marshall Loeb, was out of town, and that provided an opportunity for higher-ups to meddle. Whether acting on his own initiative or responding to orders, corporate editor Gil Rogin paid me a highly unusual visit one afternoon. His mission: to argue, in effect, that Time Inc.'s historic separation between church and state was an anachronism and that making sure Time Inc. didn't lose any advertising by publishing a harsh story was more important than ensuring that my journalistic product remained untainted. As a result of his intervention, I recall making a few cosmetic changes in the article, but I mostly stood my ground, and the article was published with its key points undisturbed. *New York* quoted a source who said, "Marshall didn't want his writer's work tinkered with. Marshall stood his ground, and the story remained intact."

The concept for this book sprang from a 2008 *Fortune* cover story titled "GM and Me." Much of the material in this book is drawn from articles I have written for *Fortune* since 1986 and, earlier, for *Time* from 1980 to 1985. For accounts of GM in the 1950s, 1960s, and 1970s, I have drawn on past issues of *Time*, as well as longer works by other authors. It is my hope that viewing Detroit through a personal lens will give readers a better understanding of the men who presided over the U.S. auto industry and add perspective to the decisions that led the industry to its current state. Unfortunately, I can't change the outcome. The decline of these companies has been a tragedy for their employees, retirees, stock-holders, dealers, suppliers, and residents of cities such as Detroit and Flint and Pontiac.

GM's failure, despite the inexorable decline of its market share, wasn't continuous. Buried within those years were outstanding careers, successful products, and periods of great prosperity. There were times when GM looked like the corporate superstar that it saw in the mirror every day and times when it looked like the clueless giant that an increasing number of its critics came to recognize. Second-guessing is easy, but I was wrong about as often as I was right in judging GM and have pointed out those occasions where I blew the call. Others may have a higher batting average writing about the business. But nobody has had more fun. Covering the past thirty years of the U.S. auto industry has been consistently engaging, challenging, and intellectually rewarding.

CHAPTER 1

GM at the Peak

O n November 1, 1954, *Time* magazine published a cover story that was so energizing and admiring that it made you want to stand up and salute its subject. Entitled "The Battle of Detroit," it described the work done by GM president and CEO Harlow Curtice to get new cars ready for the 1955 model year. In those years, *Time* was usually friendly to big business, especially those who were big advertisers. The November story was a prelude to *Time* naming Curtice Man of the Year for 1955, and it couldn't have painted him in more heroic terms if he were marching across Europe with General Patton's Third Army:

"Into a large, cluttered Detroit studio one day 18 months ago strode a trim, lean man with the suave good looks of an ambassa-dor and the cheery smile of a salesman. . . . There for inspection by Harlow H. ('Red') Curtice, president of General Motors Corp., was the topmost secret of the greatest manufacturing corporation in the world—a full-sized, blue-and-ivory clay model of the Chev-rolet for 1955."

The story went on to describe Curtice circling the clay mockup and making suggestions on how to improve its looks: a horizontal crease in the trunk molding here, a daring dip in the belt line there. After fiddling for a while, Curtice gave his approval: "That's it!" he said. His words, according to *Time*, were the signal for Chevy to spend some three hundred million dollars on the new model — the most ever.

It was a peak moment for Curtice and for GM, and especially for impressionable readers like me, at age nine, just beginning to learn about the remote corporate colossus. GM would command a majority U.S. market share that year and become the first company in history to earn a billion dollars. Curtice had started out as a bookkeeper but grew up to be a supersalesman. He developed a shrewd understanding of how design created buzz and sold cars; he doubled Buick sales when he ran the division. Curtice may have been the last GM CEO who wielded so much power in the design studio. With cars like the '57 Chevy and the '59 Cadillac designed during his tenure, the sheer power of their tail-finned good looks allowed GM to demonstrate its market dominance at every country intersection and freeway entrance. After Curtice, GM was run by bookkeepers who stayed bookkeepers, too focused on the numbers to worry much about what was coming out of the design studio.

It is not clear if Curtice was a workaholic—the term wasn't created until 1971—but like all GM executives before and since, he put in the hours. He lived in Flint, sixty miles north of Detroit, but worked, ate, and slept in the General Motors building from eight o'clock on Monday morning until late Friday evening. Then, back when GM still had airplanes, he flew home to Flint in a two-engine Lockheed Ventura. His hard work paid off. In the middle of the great stretch of prosperity after World War II, 1955 would be a record year for car sales, and GM would leave all its competitors—

not just Ford and Chrysler but also Studebaker-Packard and American Motors—behind.

Chevy led the way, with a new styling look approved by Curtice—long, low, and forward-plunging—and a hot new 265-cubic-inch V-8 engine. Talk about optimism and prosperity! The 1955 Chevy, built from the ground up to house the V-8, was nineteen feet long (today's Chevy Impala is two and a half feet shorter) and carried six passengers. You could buy a Chevy One Fifty—a stripper model with four doors—for $1,827 ($14,500 in 2009 dollars). By comparison, a 2009 Chevy Impala started at $23,790. Chevy's production during the 1955 model year production soared to 1.7 million units, a record for any manufacturer in the history of the automobile business.

It was a good year for the rest of the company as well. GM would produce more than half of all the cars sold in America—twice as many as second-place Ford, and three times more than Chrysler. By the end of the decade, Chevy alone had boosted its share of the U.S. car market to 26 percent; with Pontiac, Oldsmobile, Buick, and Cadillac added in, all of GM would grow to a 52 percent market share. In addition to being the sales leader, GM was also the pricing leader. When GM boosted prices for face-lifted three-year-old '57 models, Ford, which had earlier raised prices only 2.9 percent, was able to come back in with another boost to match it.

With that kind of market dominance, the money poured in. Between 1950 and 1955, GM's return on investment averaged a staggering 25 percent. GM was so big and so powerful that the Justice Department wanted to break it up. As its market share kept rising in a down market in 1956, the government warned that it might have to take "extreme action" unless GM checked its approaching monopoly. Washington suggested that GM could best accomplish this by divesting itself of a division or two. Besides dominating in cars, GM produced 43 percent of the nation's trucks, had built 60 percent of all the diesel engines sold in the world, and was the world's largest maker of refrigerators under the Frigidaire brand.

The government attention was well deserved. Besides being the biggest car company, GM was also the most proficient. Having passed Ford in the 1920s by offering cars that were changed every year, GM made sure it remained the styling and technology leader. Its cars of the 1950s were all new, their styling capturing the pent-up wartime desire for change with an exciting spirit bordering on the flamboyant: two-tone color schemes, outrageous fins, and high-compression V-8 engines. Curved one-piece windshields appeared in 1950. Buick and Oldsmobile and Cadillac offered power steering in 1952. "Silver streak" styling belonged to Pontiac; five bands of chrome swept over the hood and down the trunk of most models. For Chevys, the bowtie emblem was mounted on chrome-plated wings. The tailfin craze started in 1954—or 1948, depending on your point of view; in both cases, they decorated the rear ends of Cadillacs.

George Romney, president of tiny American Motors, complained that GM's huge market share and unrivaled advertising budget in effect forced its competitors to follow in its wake. Appearing at a 1956 Senate hearing on alleged monopolistic practices by GM, he said, not unreasonably, that a company doing 50 percent of the business could make an aspect of a car's appearance a requirement for product acceptance. If one of the smaller companies had put a wraparound windshield on its car, for instance, it might have been a flop, but the fact that it was put on by a company as big as GM helped make it a success. "In the field of fashion," Romney argued, "familiarity brings acceptance."

GM was a machine that kept getting bigger and stronger. By 1957, it offered dozens of body styles—two- and four-doors, station wagons, soft-top and hardtop convertibles—and hundreds of trim combinations. Despite the complexity, the company was nimble. The 1954 Oldsmobile 98, for example, required less than a year to go from concept initiation to product launch (today's cars take three to four years). Responding to radical design changes made by Chrysler in 1957, GM decided to redo the styling for all five vehicle divisions and launch them all in the 1959 model year, scrapping previous designs that had already been approved. The new lineup was at dealers less than two years after the decision was made. Each car was radically different in appearance from its 1958 model year predecessor, and each was a hit.

GM's phenomenal success seemed to set it apart from the rest of corporate America. It was in a category all of its own. Is it any wonder that in 1953, GM president Charles E. Wilson confused the national interest with GM's during his confirmation hearing as secretary of defense? Nor is it surprising that in the Eisenhower prosperity of the mid-1950s, businessmen like those at GM were treated like princes: superior creatures who bestrode the earth, creating wealth and bestowing favors. Celebrity business worship reached its peak with Lee Iacocca in the mid-1980s. But before Iacocca, there was Curtice.

Then in its heyday, *Time*, the weekly newsmagazine, used all its rhetorical skills to raise Curtice up to the status of near-sainthood. And why not? He was head of the most successful company in the history of mankind: "The man who has given General Motors its record share of the auto business looks as if he just stepped out of a Cadillac ad. . . . His bright blue eyes sparkle like a newly polished car, his smile is as broad as a Cadillac grille. His voice is quiet, his manner calm. But under the Curtice hood there throbs a machine with the tireless power of one of his own 260-h.p. engines."

During Curtice's tenure, GM's cars grew larger, acquiring bulk, getting longer wheelbases, and adding profitable accessories. "You never stand still in this business," Curtice was quoted as saying. "You either go up or down."

After Curtice, GM began to go down. Curtice was too powerful for his own good, and his very success set in motion the actions that laid the groundwork for many of GM's problems for the next half century. That's because Curtice wanted to sell more and more cars. He endlessly promoted the company and its products and spent one billion dollars to expand production. His enthusiasm got him crossways with Alfred P. Sloan, Jr., creator of the modern GM and its management system and who served as chairman for nearly thirty years. Sloan feared that Curtice had become too independent from the finance staff and that his unchecked desire to sell more cars would get GM in trouble with the trustbusters at the Justice Department. So Sloan saw to it that Curtice did not succeed him as chairman in 1956.

Instead of a car guy at the top of the company, GM got a bean counter. Fred Donner, who ascended to the top jobs with Sloan's backing in 1958, established a much different style. Donner was born in tiny (population 1,500) Three Oaks, Michigan, where his father was the accountant for the only plant in town—a featherbone factory making corsets and buggy whips. Like Curtice, Donner started as a numbers guy. But instead of working in Detroit as

Curtice did, Donner spent his entire career in New York City; he commuted to work via train and subway. Donner seldom set foot in a car factory and ran GM from an office in the old General Motors building on Columbus Circle in Manhattan. All he knew about the corporation, it was said, he learned from executive meetings, balance sheets, and reports. Numbers were his life. Meeting a young executive for the first time, he would reportedly ask afterward, "How much are we paying that man?"

A subordinate once described Donner as "short, stocky, with a stern face, [and having] all the emotion of a pancake." Donner totally lacked his predecessor's sense of flair and public relations. During a rare interview, when he was asked whether GM should ease up on the competition so as not to drive them out of business, Donner snapped: "And when did you stop beating your wife? If you are thinking of Studebaker-Packard, we didn't drive them to their present condition. They drove themselves there. Did you ever stop to wonder what they did with the profits of the lush war years, if they reinvested them in the business?"

Donner also displayed an ignorance that was to plague GM for the rest of the twentieth century and into the twenty-first: an inability to understand the public's interest in small cars and a total lack of interest in learning how to profit from them. European manufacturers, led by Volkswagen, were shipping increasing numbers of small cars to the United States during Donner's tenure, which lasted until October 31, 1967, but the accountant from Three Oaks was not interested. He had his own ideas about how to satisfy customers. It is not what people say they want, he would argue, but what they are willing to buy—often two different things. Take chrome, for example, Donner went on. People said they didn't want chrome. But in a good year GM loaded the cars with chrome, and they sold extremely well.

Donner's blunderbuss style had a purpose, according to journalist Ed Cray, author of *Chrome Colossus* (1980). "Donner was a cold-blooded financial expert, keenly aware that he did not command the esteem of the automotive divisions. Precise to a fault, he determined to whip the automotive men into line. Intolerant of dissent, Donner insisted on executive loyalty above, which eventually gutted the automotive divisions of their independence and what little creativity remained in the corporate world dominated by professional managers. One executive accused him of 'attempting to bookkeep an organization into prosperity.'"

In making the company more orderly, Donner would leave a lasting impression on GM. To centralize control of the far-flung assembly plants run by the automotive divisions, Donner took control and turned them over to the General Motors Assembly Division (GMAD). Chevrolet would never again oversee its own manufacturing facilities, which instead would turn out cars for as many as four brands under the new system. In another cost-saving measure, Donner got GM to increase the number of common parts. The family differences that had distinguished Buicks from Oldsmobiles started to disappear, and in time, so did the customers. For its part, GMAD would prove so inefficient and hard to manage that CEO Roger Smith made its dissolution a key goal of his 1984 reorganization.

Nobody knew it then, but GM was losing its grasp on public taste and would never get it back. It would struggle for another forty years to figure out a way to distinguish its different brands meaningfully while still achieving commonality of parts and economies of scale. As for small cars, they sold as much on style and on being fun to drive as they did on economy and price, and GM never did discover the secret sauce. Its list of failures is quite astounding—Corvair, Vega, Chevette, Cavalier, Cobalt—and with them came damage to its reputation that lasted for decades. Donner was the first of several GM executives who didn't have a clue. "A car," he said once, "is a whole series of engineering compromises. To get economy you have to sacrifice something else. The economy cars we have examined usually have low weight and low performance. You can't have everything." But GM's competitors could.

GM had become so big and so successful that its executives began to have trouble seeing out. They confused their view of corporate life inside GM with the actual world all around it. Donner knew what sold and what made a profit, but he didn't know his customers. By the time that his successors began to understand them, GM had lost a whole generation of buyers—with little chance of getting them back.

CHAPTER 2

Growing Up in the Car-Crazy Fifties

Coming of age in the Connecticut suburbs, I was only dimly aware of the colossus that GM had become. Fairfield County wasn't Detroit or Flint. No one in town worked in an auto factory or at a supplier, and even GM's advertising agencies were hundreds of miles away.

Cars, on the other hand, were a big deal. Everybody in the neighborhood knew when a new car showed up in somebody's driveway. This wasn't Los Angeles, so you weren't what you drove, but cars did define how you felt about yourself and how you wanted others to feel about you. GM, Ford, and Chrysler made an impact, but this affluent East Coast enclave was fertile territory for newly arriving models from England and the Continent. Mercedes and Jaguars resonated more than Cadillacs and Lincolns.

All of this I observed mostly at a distance. Although I grew up in Greenwich, then as now one of the richest communities in the United States, the Taylor family operated on thinner margins. Since our funds were not unlimited, my parents had to choose where we spent our money. Private schools for five children took top priority, followed by family vacations and sailing lessons. Signaling to friends and neighbors our interest in automobiles was not a priority.

I got my first exposure to a General Motors product in 1952. My father wasn't much of a car guy—spending money on anything wasn't part of his MO—but he did consider himself a shrewd buyer. Shopping for a car brought out the best of his bargain-hunting instincts. One summer day, I was sitting on the front step of our home in the Byram neighborhood when a new Chevrolet Deluxe two-door was delivered. Color: brown. Price: $1,696.

Our family, then numbering five, would continue to grow, so this would be our one and only two-door. All the rest would be station wagons. The Chevy didn't turn many heads, but as I recall, it mostly provided reliable transportation. Except when it wouldn't start or when my father had to lie underneath it to affix tire chains for rear-drive traction in the snow. He ran a sporting goods store in New York City that sold skis, and we had become a family of skiers. One memorable Sunday night on the way back from Vermont, the Chevy stopped running near Hartford. Somehow we found a garage with a mechanic on duty. He opened the hood, climbed into the engine compartment, and squirted some sort of flammable liquid into the carburetor. Flames shot up but the car started, and we went on our way. Another time, the roof-top ski rack collapsed under a full load of skis, and we stuffed the equipment inside the car for a crowded five-hour drive back from Vermont.

Greenwich was a far cry from the super-money hedge-fund haven it became before the crash of 2009. It felt almost Victorian in those days. My mother had grown up in town, and my grandmother and great-grandmother still lived nearby. White-gloved policemen directed traffic at intersections on Greenwich Avenue (they still do), while parking rules were enforced by another policeman driving a three-wheeled motorcycle. In lieu of parking meters, he would chalk the rear tires of cars to see which had stayed too long in a space.

Old Greenwich, the part of town where we moved in 1952, was quieter still. Founded as a beach community on Long Island Sound, and originally called Sound Beach, it was strongly influenced by the water. Our house was one block away on Shore Road, which at its other end led directly to the town's public beach. In this environment of families and boats, Ford, not GM, held sway. For many years, the Ford Country Squire station wagon, with metal sides resembling wood trim, was the car of choice, preferably personalized with painted initials on the door or plastic marine signal flags. GM didn't seem to have a contender in the wood-panel-wagon category. Buicks were considered acceptable, but Cadillacs were avoided as ostentatious.

Still, the idea of a big, powerful General Motors was implanted in my brain. In addition to the *Saturday Evening Post, Time* made a weekly appearance in our Republican household, and as a compulsive reader, I was picking it up and making my way from "Sport" and "TV-Radio" in the back of the magazine to "Nation" and "Business" closer to the front. At some point, the selection of Harlow Curtice as 1955's Man of the Year must have registered on my developing consciousness. It would have been difficult for it not to have. *Time* described Curtice as "first among scores of equals," a businessman "whose skill, daring and foresight are forever opening new frontiers for the expanding American economy." For his part, Curtice told the magazine, "General Motors must always lead."

Working for the auto company sounded almost like a patriotic calling. For awhile, when people asked me what I wanted to be when I grew up, I told them that I wanted to be chairman of General Motors. I think I learned the word "martini" at the same time. It would be many years before I would have a direct connection with either.

Our family turned out not to be loyal GM customers, as my father, seemingly oblivious to fashion and status but devoted to saving a buck, scoured the automotive landscape for bargains. Sloan's concept that customers would trade up from Chevy to Oldsmobile and Buick and then to Cadillac as their means improved didn't resonate with Dad. In 1955, he picked up a Ford Ranch Wagon (six cylinders, two doors, no fake wood) at the end of the model year (cheaper that way if you didn't take into account the depreciation that occurred when the model year changed). The Ford was painted sea-foam green (popular that year and a good choice). There were no seat belts, of course, and on trips to faraway places like Vermont and Maine, the wagon's rear seats would be folded down and my brother, sister, and I would be laid in the back like so many sticks of wood.

In 1958, Dad shifted manufacturers again and invested in a brown Plymouth Deluxe Suburban station wagon—the base trim level, as usual. It seemed like a timely choice. Plymouth was enjoying a renaissance owing to its adoption the previous year of "Forward Look" styling, whose most prominent element was rather preposterous tailfins. The Plymouth had two notable features: its third seat had been turned 180 degrees and faced the rear, and it could be accessed by a tailgate with an electric window. It also had a manual transmission with the gear lever on the steering column—three on the tree.

The novelty of the rear seat soon wore thin, but the matter of the gear shift loomed large. Operating a manual transmission required more skill than an automatic; it was the difference between driving and just steering. I had turned sixteen, and this would be the car in which I would be tested to get my driver's license. After a few weeks of driver's ed, I passed my driving test on the first try (no parallel parking required). Like most beginning drivers, I wasn't any good and acquired my first traffic ticket within a month for running a stop sign that I never saw. On one of my first evenings out, I sideswiped the personal car of an off-duty Greenwich policeman and left the scene of the accident. I endured a harsh verbal rebuke from him underneath the open bedroom window of my parents.

Meanwhile, I was acquiring much of my automotive knowledge from my younger brother John. He was more tuned in to the local car culture—what was cool and what was merely acceptable. That kind of knowledge came from hanging around playgrounds and parking lots, something that had little appeal for me. He was also more aware of the Porsches, Mercedes, MGs, and Austin Healys that were arriving in town. Close to New York, relatively affluent, and full of trendsetters, Greenwich was fertile ground for the new and different.

As it turned out, I wasn't destined to log many miles in the Plymouth. Besides being big and ungainly, its shift linkage tended to seize up after the engine got hot, requiring us to pop the hood and shake the rods loose, protecting our hands to keep from being burned. My father, meanwhile, saw another opportunity to save money. As first I, and then my brother, started to drive, he sensibly decided to acquire a series of used cars that would absorb the inevitable dings and dents. Many of them were second-tier European brands that weren't very reliable, but maybe that was the point— we weren't being encouraged to set off on any cross-country trips. I recall driving an old blue Vauxhall over a rock that dented the undercarriage and calling a tow truck after I ran out of gas on the Connecticut Turnpike. My brother kept pace by allowing a white Corvair to roll backward down a hill and into a tree after dropping off a date because he forgot to set the hand brake.

The first car I ever owned was a black 1961 Volkswagen Beetle I purchased for six hundred dollars when I turned twenty-one. It was a safe choice identity-wise, since my college campus in Vermont was crawling with VWs. And except for the lack of a fuel gauge, which caused me to run out of gas a few times, and a disinclination to start when the humidity was high, it served me reliably for two years. It was replaced by a red Volvo 544, the humpbacked model that looked like a 1940 Ford, which served me less reliably in graduate school. The Volvo failed to start at all in the wintertime, and by the time I sold it, it had a passenger door that would fly open when I drove around corners. It was a bad experience that left me feeling cool toward Volvos for the next forty years.

My aspirations to become GM's chairman faded away about the time I discovered *Mad* magazine, and my career goals remained fuzzy after that. Three-quarters of the way through college, though, I was lucky enough to land a summer job writing news for a local radio station in Bridgeport, Connecticut. It was miles from a major market, but the station had a history of grooming up-and-coming broadcast news people for jobs at CBS.

The four young men I worked with that summer—all recent college grads—seemed smart and savvy about the world and loved their work, despite our cramped newsroom on the second floor of a battery factory. Even though I had to arrive at the office at six in the morning, I loved it, too, the adrenaline rush that came from meeting a deadline every thirty minutes during morning and afternoon drive time. I had been worried about being bored by work, especially when faced by a lifetime of it. Here, I thought, was a career where I would always be stimulated.

So after college and graduate journalism school, I set out to become a network TV correspondent. Cutting your teeth in the hinterlands was supposed to be the ticket to advancement, so I went to work as a reporter at an NBC affiliate in Terre Haute, Indiana. To celebrate my first full-time job, I replaced my troublesome Volvo with an even more troublesome MGB.

It shocks me to recall this, but in those pre-Internet days, everything I knew about cars I had learned from my brother or picked up on the street. I read nothing—not even *Road & Track*—and consulted no one about my purchase. There was no J.D. Power and Associates or Edmunds.com to provide third-party guidance, and *Consumer Reports* wasn't rating sports cars.

I should have known better than to get involved with an MG with as little aptitude or interest as I had in things mechanical. Although MG had progressed to roll-up windows by then, the B had an antique canvas roof held in place with struts and snaps that I occasionally had to assemble in a driving rain. Besides consuming about a third of my take-home pay with monthly payments, it also conspired to consume another third in repair bills. The electrical system was a big problem, as were the batteries that hung down behind the back seat and were exposed to the elements. Then there was the time I had to cut off one of the lovely though anachronistic wire wheels because it had become fused on the axle hub after I neglected to grease it.

Eight months in Terre Haute was long enough, and I moved from the hundredth largest market to another NBC affiliate in the thirty-seventh largest one in Grand Rapids. I found an apartment close to the office for those days when the MG wouldn't start.

In those days, General Motors was so large and diverse that it sprawled across lower Michigan. Buick's home was in Flint, and Oldsmobile's was in Lansing. Grand Rapids, the furniture capital, wasn't associated with any particular division, but as the second largest city in the state, it couldn't escape GM. It was home to three GM parts plants, all represented by the United Auto Workers, as well as dozens of smaller parts suppliers.

One gloomy afternoon in the early 1970s, a smallish man in a gray suit came to town to hold a news conference. His name was Richard Gerstenberg, and it turned out that he was about to take over as chairman and CEO of General Motors. An accountant by training, he got his first job at GM keeping track of employee time-cards and worked his way up from there. He would always refer to himself as "Old Dick the Bookkeeper." Gerstenberg had a short tenure at the top, retiring in November 1974 after less than three years, but he remained on the board of directors after stepping down, as was the practice in those days, until May 1980.

"Gerstenberg was the paradigm of General Motors executives,"

writes Ed Cray. "He was cautious, colorless, virtually unknown beyond the confines of the industry, and a diplomat who brokered
adroit compromises between factions on the fourteenth floor."
That made him part of a system that perpetuated the company but
did not admit much in the way of fresh air. In Gerstenberg's esti-
mation, it didn't need any. "We have the best people in this or any
industry," Gerstenberg told a group of employees in November
1972. "I always feel a special personal pride, a General Motors
pride, because I am one of you, a General Motors man."

Years later I saw Gerstenberg at a GM event in New York City.
By then eighty years old and shrunken in stature, he shyly introduced himself to Bob Stempel, who was then president. The scene
stuck with me. Though still a GM man, Gerstenberg seemed in-
significant without the corporate apparatus behind him. Mere
men, even a former chairman and CEO, were nothing compared
with the might of the company.

As I was about to learn firsthand, because Detroit was beckon-
ing. Eight years in broadcast journalism had convinced me that I
wasn't going to be the next Roger Mudd. So I began freelance writing and managed to place several articles with the *Free Press* in
Detroit, 160 miles to the east. In 1977, the newspaper offered me
a job. Not in the city room covering politics, as I had hoped—I was
too green for that—but in the business section, where they could
keep an eye on me.

Detroit was not a place where I had ever thought about living
or had any connection with, but it provided journalistic opportunities I never imagined. With a daily circulation of 629,961, the *Free
Press* was the sixth-largest newspaper in the United States. Detroit
had been badly scarred by race riots in 1967 and the recession of

1973, and white residents were fleeing the city, but it was still a great news town. The *Free Press* business section, consisting of six writers, one copy editor, an editor, and a secretary, was physically isolated from the rest of the news operation and developed its own culture and habits, mostly good ones. Journalists with national aspirations still passed through Detroit in those days, and I shared office space with award-winning reporters such as Clark Hoyt, who later joined the *New York Times* and *Fortune's* own Allan Sloan.

Being new to the newspaper and to newspapering, I didn't qualify for the auto beat, but cars and car culture were all around, and so, soon after sticking my toe in the water, I was swimming in the deep end. Detroit was the Motor City. You couldn't see much evidence of the Big Three in local politics, and Detroit's sports teams were in a league of their own, but the car companies permeated everything else in town, and GM stood above all.

CHAPTER 3

Cracks in GM's Edifice

GM has an embarrassment of riches," *Time* declared in March 1962. "With Frederic Donner, a tack-sharp onetime accountant, as chairman, G.M. now commands 55.7% of the U.S.-made auto market. That is a company record, the highest in the industry since Henry Ford's model Ts got 60% in 1921, and more than enough to prompt some nervous glances from G.M. officials toward the U.S. Justice Department. . . . Chevy alone has captured 33% of the market."

In fact, by the 1960s, GM had stopped growing by several key measures. Its U.S. market share peaked in 1962 and started falling after that (for the first half of 2009, it was 19 percent). GM's overall net profit margin had reached a postwar high of 11.5 percent thirteen years earlier in 1949. The value of the company as measured by its market capitalization was declining, too. GM's stock price peaked in 1965. As the company entered bankruptcy in June 2009, its shares were effectively worthless.

At the moment when it should have been building success upon success, GM started to make mistakes—bad ones. The cracks appeared first in its public image, but the fissures went deeper than that. The immediate cause of each incident—the flawed Corvair, the botched Nader investigation, the unfortunate Chevymobile—was different, but the underlying cause was that GM couldn't cope with prosperity. Lacking any real competition, the company turned inward. It produced a generation of leaders from the financial staff who were concerned more with process than with product. Alfred P. Sloan, the wise man, knew where GM's biggest threats lay. "Success, however, may bring self-satisfaction," he wrote. "The spirit of venture is lost in the inertia of the mind against change." But Sloan had retired in 1956, and there was no one of comparable stature to make sure that GM stayed on the right course.

The sorry saga of the Chevrolet Corvair illustrates a lot of what went wrong with GM in the 1960s. The car's engineering was compromised by shortsighted financial considerations, which led to mechanical problems that GM first disputed and then acknowledged only reluctantly. Following that, the company tried to silence the car's most vocal critic, a decision that still reverberates today. With the possible exception of Ford and the Edsel, it is impossible to think of another company whose missteps with a single product have stuck to it as doggedly as the Corvair fiasco has stuck to GM.

The import-fighter with an innovative air-cooled rear engine was launched with great fanfare in 1959. Spearheaded by engineer Edward N. Cole, who later rose to president, the Corvair was GM's first effort in a forty-year struggle to build a competitive small car. Unfortunately, the finance staff had ruled against the installation of a fifteen-dollar stabilizer bar, so the Corvair was prone to mishaps because the rear wheels had a tendency to buckle during high-speed turns. When accidents, along with lawsuits, began to proliferate, GM was called to Capitol Hill to explain what was happening. As would happen again and again, GM did not distinguish itself when thrust into the national spotlight. Under questioning from Senators Abraham Ribicoff of Connecticut and Edward Kennedy of Massachusetts, Chairman and CEO Donner—the accountant with the steel-trap mind—appeared to be unable to recall how much GM had earned the year before. He had to ask an aide before he came up with the $1.7 billion number.

Despite its shortcomings, the Corvair continued to sell respectably for several years until a young lawyer named Ralph Nader appeared on the scene. In 1965 Nader published a book entitled *Unsafe at Any Speed* that exposed a list of safety and mechanical problems with the Corvair that went beyond the stabilizer bar. Nader made three main complaints: the Corvair was unsafe on turns; the cooling system leaked carbon monoxide fumes; and in a front-end crash, a driver could be speared by the steering wheel.

Under attack by Nader, GM behaved like a Hollywood caricature of the evil, all-powerful corporation. Unbeknown to its top executives, an outside law firm retained by GM hired private investigators to tail Nader and dig up compromising information about him. The investigation soon became public, but GM committed the cardinal error of telling only part of the truth. In its initial statement about the investigation in March 1966, GM said that the Nader inquiry had been limited to his professional qualifications, background, and association with other attorneys handling the Corvair suits. The inquiry was nothing out of the ordinary, in other words.

As it turned out, the probe was far from ordinary. GM's hired investigators had interviewed nearly sixty of Nader's friends and associates and questioned why a thirty-two-year-old man with adequate means should remain unmarried. Eventually, GM president

James Roche, who had known nothing about the investigation, was forced to apologize publicly to Nader at a congressional hearing and to concede the existence of defects in the Corvair (Donner was traveling and could not appear). "I am not here to excuse, condone or justify in any way," said Roche abjectly in an appearance before the Ribicoff subcommittee. "To the extent that General Motors bears responsibility, I want to apologize here and now." He went on to say, "I deplore the kind of harassment to which Mr. Nader has apparently been subjected. As president of General Motors, I hold myself fully responsible for any action authorized or initiated by an officer of the corporation which may have any bearing on the incidents related to our investigation."

GM settled an invasion of privacy suit by Nader for $425,000. It finally added a stabilizer bar to the Corvair to reduce the likelihood of rollovers, but the car's reputation was irreparably damaged. GM sold 1.5 million Corvairs before the Senate hearings and 125,000 in four years after that. Production was discontinued in 1969.

The fallout from Nader and the Corvair was longer lived than anyone could imagine. As GM struggled to build public support in 2009 for federal loan guarantees from the Obama administration, the Nader affair from four decades earlier was raised again and again. Because of its once apparent invulnerability and omniscience, bad news seemed to stick to GM more persistently than to most companies—perhaps more than any company. It was as if the New York Yankees had been caught cheating. How could this happen to a company that was so big and so successful?

In a contemporary account, *Time* provided its own analysis of GM's reputational woes. It reported in 1970 that "critics tend to find it [GM] a distant, impersonal corporation." Over the years,

GM would spend billions of dollars to create the image of a company that behaved as if doing good was synonymous with doing well. It never quite succeeded. To this day, GM executives complain that its reputation lags behind its corporate achievements, that potential customers don't understand how good GM cars and trucks really are.

Communications aside, symptoms of corporate hardening of the arteries were appearing at GM's Detroit headquarters, where the top executives worked. Later generations of GM'ers would come to believe that the company's problems started there. "By the 1970s, the 'fourteenth floor' had come to be viewed as the inner sanctum," write the anonymous authors of a GM internal history, published in 2000 by the company's history project. "And it was making decisions under the same basic structure Sloan had put in place fifty years earlier. Decision-making, monitoring, and measurements by policy committees and staffs had come to be viewed and accepted as 'the GM way'—as had the practice of often circumventing the process to maintain divisional independence. Effective as the structure had been in its prime, it was not suited to the changing competitive realities of the 1980s and 1990s, where speed and agility were much more crucial than in prior decades."

On the occasions when I visited the old corporate headquarters (which GM abandoned in 1996 for more modern accommodations in downtown Detroit), I was struck by the vast space—wide corridors, enormous secretarial offices—the library-like hush, and the lack of human contact. Where were the water coolers or copying machines where executives could gather and informally share information? Analyst, consultant, author, and longtime GM critic Maryann Keller had a similar reaction when she visited. "When the elevator arrives, you encounter two sets of electronically locked glass doors. . . . Once inside, the first thing you notice is the deafening silence. No bustling workers racing by with reams of paper. No heated voices raised. Everyone on the floor. . . work[s] behind closed doors, each of them laboring through a voluminous pile of paperwork. . . . If a conversation with another executive is desired, an appointment is made by phone through his secretary—even if he's right next door."

The men who occupied these offices seemed almost as gray as their surroundings. In the spring of 1970, Fred Donner had reached down into the organization to tap Gersternberg, "Old Dick the Bookkeeper," to be vice chairman, and named Treasurer Thomas Aquinas Murphy as vice president of car and truck production. It was like a lame-duck president nominating justices for the Supreme Court who would remain on the bench long after his term had ended. The company's methodical system of promotion from within meant that Donner had effectively selected the men who would lead GM for the next decade. Years after Donner was gone, his acolytes from the finance staff would continue to influence GM policy. Donner's moves also underscored GM's shift from an industrial company that made things to a finance operation whose primary preoccupation was making money.

After stepping down as CEO, Donner himself would remain on GM's board of directors until reaching the mandatory retirement age of seventy—allowing him to second-guess the actions of his successor. The board was packed with other insiders, too. When Donner left office, twelve of the board's twenty members were GM officers or retirees. That's hardly a way to aerate a company with fresh ideas. (In 2009, Chairman and CEO Rick Wagoner was the only insider on a fourteen-person board. Of course, that didn't prevent complaints about a rubber-stamp board that was too protective of Wagoner. Several of its members were retired CEOs, for whom GM was a source of significant income and prestige.)

Beneath the board, GM had become encrusted with a committee-and-meeting system that slowed everything to a crawl and made smart decision-making all but impossible. Then an up-and-coming engineer, John Z. DeLorean recounted an exchange at an executive meeting in which a minor point of compensation was being discussed. (The incident is described in DeLorean's autobiography.) CEO Gerstenberg suddenly barked: "We can't make a decision on this now. I think we ought to form a task force to look into this and come back with a report in 90 to 120 days." After an eerie silence, according to DeLorean, a soon-to-retire executive vice president spoke up: "Dick, this presentation is the result of the task force you appointed some time ago. Most of the people you just appointed to the new task force are on the old one."

Still, GM looked remarkably successful from the outside (Ford and Chrysler had their own problems), and many observers had come to believe that this success was owing to the strength of GM's management. As the industry leader, GM attracted talented people and retained them through a combination of tradition, salary, and delayed bonuses that would be forfeited if they quit. But GM personnel management was becoming as dysfunctional as its system of policy committees and staffs. For one thing, it was rare for anyone at GM to be fired. For another, the company's practice of promoting high-potential executives every eighteen months meant that in this long-lead business managers had moved on to their next job before problems surfaced. Executives would rise through the ranks, leaving their wakes strewn with failures for which their successors were held responsible.

In the era of giant institutions such as IBM, AT&T, and Sears, a self-perpetuating corporate apparatus like GM's was seen as a positive attribute. As a young journalist, I had certainly found it impressive. I wrote admiringly for the Detroit *Free Press* in 1978 about GM's "black book" of management succession. The book listed the one thousand top jobs in the company and contained the names of people who held them, as well as those of people who might one day succeed them. In all there were about five thousand names, representing 4 or 5 percent of GM's salaried workforce. Access to the black book was closely held. GM's seven executive committee members, each of whom had been with the company for at least twenty-five years, each had a copy.

Reading about the black book today makes GM leaders sound like a college of cardinals, deciding among themselves who would move up the ladder and who wouldn't. The process explained why collegiality and predictability took precedence over creativity or willingness to depart from the status quo. Yet you would have had to have been a lot more perceptive than I was to perceive the company's flaws in the 1970s because the facade was so imposing. Despite the Corvair fiasco, GM was still selling millions of cars and making billions of dollars—ergo, it must be a successful company.

The longer I covered GM, the more I began to suspect that GM's people really weren't that good; it was the company's success that made them look good. Encountering GM executives in retirement was always disconcerting for me, because they seemed like hollow men, shorn of purpose once they left the company. And executives who departed before retirement to work elsewhere were seldom able to recapture the success they had found at GM. The corporation had propped them up and supported them; when it was removed, they collapsed like rag dolls.

Part of their weakness was due to the culture in which they worked. It gives new meaning to the term "yes men." According to corporate governance experts Monks and Minow, GM employees were expected to display unwavering loyalty and behave like team players. This meant that they never questioned a decision, never contradicted a boss, and conformed to the corporate stereotype. This rigid culture was matched by a torturous decision-making process. Decisions were shuttled higher and higher up in the organization so that if anything went wrong, nobody would ever take the blame.

The old GM building on West Grand Boulevard in Detroit, with its four massive wings, reinforced the image of seniority, success, and solidity. Here, surely, was a company built for the ages. It wasn't until much later that someone pointed out to me a feature of the exterior that provided a clue about the transitory nature of corporate success. It was a discrete carved escutcheon with the letter "D." That was "D" for William Crapo Durant, GM's mercurial founder, who had planned the building before he lost control of the company for the second time in 1923. Durant, an undisciplined speculator, himself went bankrupt four times and spent his final years in his hometown of Flint, running a bowling alley and subsisting on handouts from former colleagues, including Alfred Sloan. Rick Wagoner used to joke about worrying that he would wind up broke like Durant. He didn't, but the company did.

With Donner's numbers guys in charge, GM in the 1960s and

1970s was gradually slowing down. Among the finance people, the understanding was that an engineer, left to his own devices, would spend limitless amounts of money in pursuit of the ultimate car, and it was important for them to keep the engineers in check. They did, and GM's product development efforts, charged with the impossible job of satisfying five independent divisions, gradually ground to a halt. The effect of the finance staff oversight was like putting sand in a gearbox.

The cars began to lose their flair. Under chief stylist Harley Earl, GM designs of the 1950s—especially the high-trim models—reflected the ambition and optimism of the decade. From the statuesque Chevys, including the overlooked Impala with its sweeping gull wings on the rear fascia, up through the powerful Pontiac Bonnevilles and the magnificent late 1950s Cadillacs—there was hardly a boring car in the bunch. But the chrome came off after the 1958 models, and when Bill Mitchell succeeded Earl in 1959, it marked the end of the tailfin era. Mitchell was a talented stylist in his own right; the 1954 Corvette he created was an instant classic. But once he took charge, GM design seemed to lose its way.

You got the sense of design by committee. The various pieces—front end, roof, taillights—didn't work together. Take a look again at the 1959 Pontiac with its "blade airfoil roof" that over hangs the 180-degree panoramic rear window. The car has all the appeal of a 1950s tract ranch house. Even Chevys got strange looking, with overbearing dual headlamp structures and large, teardrop-shaped taillights. Cadillac somehow avoided the chrome diet other models got, and its cars were festooned with shiny metal. Like Churchill's pudding, GM's cars lacked a theme. Only the '63 Buick Riviera from that era has a style that is admired today.

The rest of GM was sagging, too. GM's product development cycles in the 1960s, which had been among the shortest, were becoming among the longest in the industry, according to GM's own in-house history. More content dictated by federal regulations was part of the problem. But Mitchell's team was creating complex designs that were difficult to engineer and often even harder to manufacture. More and more unique models were being added to the mix, which stretched engineering resources. And the decision-making process, which still followed the original Sloan committee structure, had grown increasingly complex.

Another holdover from the Sloan era, powerful divisions like Buick and Cadillac competing against each other, was causing problems, too. Durant had assembled the company from individual manufacturers, and up until the 1970s, each division operated its own engineering, manufacturing, sales, and marketing activities. That put executives in charge of GM's brands in the position of fighting one another for resources and rewards rather than competing against Ford and Chrysler. Enormous amounts of energy were focused on intracompany rivalries.

That competition had surprisingly far-reaching consequences. Mountains of market data were accumulated in the individual divisions, but the company had no means of integrating the information. A corporate market research division that could provide data to all the divisions wasn't formed until 1985. Having proved itself the industry leader, GM seemed to feel no need to look beyond its own borders to investigate consumer trends. Its blindness to the world outside its doors was a recipe for parochialism, and GM would spend years trying to escape it.

Bill Hoglund, who held high-level jobs at Pontiac, Saturn, and the central office in the 1980s and 1990s, got a chance to watch the divisional rivalry firsthand. He was a rare—and often ignored—beacon of common sense at the top of the company for two decades. Hoglund grew up in the industry—his father was a GM vice president—but he was educated at Princeton and possessed a polish and perspective infrequently seen elsewhere in the organization. Earlier in his career, he made his signal contribution when he led a revival of Pontiac under the "We build excitement" slogan. But Hoglund's frequent outbreaks of twenty-twenty vision didn't sit well with higher-ups, and his career stalled just below the top rung. "After I ran Saturn, Roger [Smith] didn't know what to do with me," he told me once, and he was shunted off to head the parts division that eventually was spun off from GM as Delphi Corporation. Later he served as Jack Smith's consigliere in 1992 when Smith took over the company.

Journalists loved Hoglund because of his obvious sincerity and his willingness to stray from the corporate line. I valued the time spent with him, so much so that he became my first kidnapped GM executive. At an East Coast event staged to launch the Pontiac Fiero in 1984, I pummeled him with questions as we drove out of New York City in another two-seat car, preventing him from following the directions in the route book. We wound up on the wrong side of the Hudson River in upstate New York and were an hour late for lunch.

Hoglund was an astute observer of GM culture. He demonstrated it in an interview for GM's internal history when he described what he saw as the beginning of brand overlap and divisional confusion. His account neatly illustrates the problems that arise in corporations when they become too inwardly focused. Faced with a rare challenge from Ford, Chevy abruptly decided to move upscale. "It was about the time of the 1965 Chevrolet Caprice," Hoglund said. "Before that we had a fairly well defined product strategy. But Ford had come out with what they called at the time their LTD. It forced Chevrolet to come up with an answer, which was the Caprice—essentially a Chevrolet with a Cadillac-like grille and a little better trim. It was in a sense a cheap Cadillac. And so you've got a Chevrolet priced up there in the mid-size Buick, Oldsmobile, and Pontiac range. And from there on it was 'Katie bar the door.' We didn't really have any systems to make sure that the divisions weren't tripping over each other."

The strange career of corporate maverick John DeLorean said volumes about the company—and not a little about DeLorean. The 1960s and 1970s were a time of experimentation with grooming, clothes, and behavior, but not at GM, where gray suits still reigned. Amid the corporate conformity, DeLorean, a good-looking man, stood out with his long hair, sideburns, and young girl-friends. DeLorean wasn't all about appearance; he had scored some legitimate business successes. He became part of a team that strengthened Pontiac and was credited with creating the muscle car by stuffing a big engine into a lightweight Pontiac Tempest body and calling it the GTO.

He also took an adolescent's delight in flouting company rules. Bill Hoglund, who worked for DeLorean, was quoted in *Automotive News*, a trade weekly, describing DeLorean's less than diligent work habits. "He would leave the office on Thursday afternoon, and you wouldn't see him again until Tuesday morning." Hoglund later learned that DeLorean was taking a company plane for long weekends with his girlfriend to a hotel room that had been stocked with goodies, at company expense, by district officials. DeLorean squandered money on a prototype of a Chevrolet limousine because he wanted to ride around in one. He also spent twice the allowable budget to redecorate his office. Another executive, Jim McDonald, who went on to serve as president under Roger Smith, recalled DeLorean giving his (DeLorean's) hair stylist a GM company car that the company had a hard time retrieving after DeLorean left the company.

By this time, DeLorean had acquired a huge public profile and had risen to within a few rungs of the top of the corporation. But his shenanigans finally got to be too much, and CEO Murphy pushed DeLorean out of his $650,000-a-year job as group executive for cars and trucks in 1974. Publicly, it was called a retirement, and most people believed it. No one could grasp the notion that a star like DeLorean would lose a job at GM.

I met DeLorean a couple of years later, after a book appeared that he had coauthored and then disowned before publication. A kiss-and-tell story of GM in the 1960s and 1970s, it seemed scandalous then but rings all too true today. Titled *On a Clear Day You Can See General Motors*, it depicts senior GM executives as men hemmed in by tradition, swamped in paperwork, and totally in thrall to their company careers. "The path to the top required a cultivated subservience," wrote DeLorean. "It was called 'kiss-my-assing' when it was done by a supplier to a customer, and 'loyalty' when it was done inside GM."

Subordinates were treated like lackeys. Pete Estes, then Pontiac's chief engineer, complained to DeLorean during a trip to San Francisco: "Why the hell wasn't someone out to meet me at the airport. You knew I was coming but there was nobody there. I served my time picking up my bosses at the airport." Ranking executives, DeLorean said, made every effort to have their meal checks and other expenses picked up by subordinates so that if shareholders inquired at the annual meeting, the brass could boast of modest expense accounts.

Despite GM's public probity, spying on competitors was not unknown, according to DeLorean. He revealed that in the early 1960s, Chevrolet had two moles working in Ford's product-planning area. "For a price," he said, they "passed on new product information." GM needed ideas from the outside, he went on, because invention and flair had disappeared from GM, which "has not had a significant technical innovation since the automatic transmission" years earlier.

In his most serious charge, DeLorean contended that GM knew about the safety problems of the Chevrolet Corvair before production began and failed to remedy them. Claimed DeLorean: "Charlie Chayne, vice president of engineering, along with his staff, took a very strong stand against the Corvair as an unsafe car long before it went on sale in 1959. He was not listened to but instead told in effect: 'You're not a member of the team. Shut up or go looking for another job.'" DeLorean wrote that he feels that the decision makers were "not immoral men." But, he added, "These same men in a business atmosphere, where everything is reduced to costs, profit goals and production deadlines, were able as a group to approve a product that most of them would not have considered approving as individuals."

DeLorean still was a good-looking man when I met him in 1979 and had lost none of his desire for attention—a poster-size picture of him, shirtless, with his young son hung in his New York office—but nothing else about him was out of the ordinary. He didn't seem like much of a revolutionary to me, but at GM—where conformity was everything and rebellion was frowned on—they never forgot him, and for years his name continued to come up in conversation and in corporate histories. Like many others, he faded after he left GM. The sports car company he started was no more successful than some GM models of the era. It collapsed in a swamp of lawsuits, and he was arrested in 1982 for drug trafficking (he was later acquitted of those charges). The last time I saw him, he was sitting on a bench in New York's Central Park, seemingly in no hurry to be anywhere in particular.

At least DeLorean had a flair for public relations. Everything that GM touched in the public arena in that era seemed to be radioactive. It didn't help that GM executives, rather than owning up to problems, tried to swat them away like so many troublesome gnats. GM'ers would prematurely announce that they had solved a problem and then have to backpedal furiously when it became clear they had done no such thing. A couple of years after the Nader affair, quality glitches with its cars were surfacing, but Roche's successor, Dick Gerstenberg, was in denial. "Proud, confident but somewhat irritated, General Motors Chairman Richard Gerstenberg has been running his own campaign to counter the bad publicity tied to the company's recent rash of auto recalls," *Time* reported. "We build them better—much better," Gerstenberg concluded. Perhaps he spoke too soon. One day later, Chevy got a recall notice for the Vega, the third in three months. GM would continue to insist on its improving quality for the rest of the twentieth century and into the twenty-first, but its claims don't resonate any better today—and the quality is still bad by some measures, worse than the Asians' or even Ford's.

It isn't surprising that the top executives were out of touch; they seemed to exist in a bubble. When I got to Detroit in 1977, Chairman and CEO Tom Murphy, the former treasurer, and President Pete Estes presided over GM like Olympian gods. Both were imposing men; Murphy was more reserved, while Estes radiated bonhomie. The only time I met them was for what turned out to be an extended photo op—one unimaginable in today's time-compressed corporate schedules. CEO Murphy, President Estes, and four other members of GM's executive committee sat for ninety minutes while six college students told them what was wrong with U.S. business. The students, from the University of Toledo and California State Polytechnic University–Pomona, had conducted a public opinion survey on the topic and somehow gained an audience with GM's top brass to give them the results.

The students lectured GM about free-market competition, improving the quality of their products, and giving customers honest information. The last message carried a special sting for GM, which was even then fending off lawsuits from customers who had bought Oldsmobiles only to discover they had been equipped with engines labeled "Chevrolet." GM blamed the bait and switch on a shortage of appropriate engines; the media immediately labeled the mismatched cars "Chevymobiles." When asked about the issue, Murphy seemed uncomprehending. "In our zeal to serve customers, we didn't tell purchasers where their engines were manufactured," he told the students. Then he added, astoundingly for a company that spent millions every year persuading buyers that Oldsmobiles represented a step up from Chevy: "We didn't think it was important."

Still, Murphy did seem to understand that GM needed to improve its public image. "We know how important our credibility is. Giving the consumer what he wants," he went on, is the best way to improve society. When the session was over, the courtly and ever diplomatic Murphy told the undergrads: "I like the way your minds work. We need more dialogue with students." If GM ever engaged in it, there is no visible evidence.

Satirists like Michael Moore found GM an easy target. In the 1989 documentary *Roger and Me*, filmmaker Michael Moore went back to his hometown of Flint, Michigan, to gauge the impact of GM's layoffs and to attempt to meet the chairman Roger Smith to "talk things over." The movie was an instant sensation, but GM never got the joke. Moore's farce would have fallen flat if Smith had actually taken Moore up on his offer, but he or his advisers declined to meet with him. When it came to sensing the climate of public opinion, GM was clueless.

Even GM's well-intentioned efforts to do the right thing had a way of blowing up in the company's face. In the 1990s, GM developed a battery-powered car to meet California's zero-emissions regulations and offered it for lease in California and Arizona. When it became clear that, despite GM's best intentions, the car wasn't economically viable or even functionally very useful—its range was limited to seventy miles—California repealed its zero-emissions requirement, and GM recalled the thousand or so cars it had built and eventually recycled them. Despite its expensive pioneering efforts, GM was flayed by environmentalists and held up for public scorn in another documentary, *Who Killed the Electric Car?* which appeared in 2006.

In fact, GM's problems with environmentalists went back to the earliest days of the movement in the 1970s. The oil crisis of 1973 provided the first signs that nineteen-foot-long cars with monster V-8 engines that got twelve miles to the gallon had been rendered obsolete. Such signs would reappear with greater urgency over the next thirty-five years, but GM mostly ignored them. Although it did eventually make its cars less hefty, GM persistently hoped the surges in popularity of small cars were passing fads. "People like big cars," said Dick Gerstenberg. "The bulk of the people who buy a car want comfort and convenience and they are willing to pay for it."

Because of its lack of corporate commitment, GM couldn't make a decent small car to save itself. Beginning in 1959 with the Corvair, each succeeding decade brought another unsuccessful small car. Each was heralded as a major breakthrough when it came out, and each was hobbled by mechanical defects, lack of market acceptance, or both. In each case, improvements were made in the vehicles, but they were all eventually canceled and GM's reputation got some more dings.

Looking back, it is now clear that GM was on a downward path from the 1960s on. But journalists, including myself, were forever discovering glimmers of hope—a good financial quarter here, a hot new model there—that would give reason for optimism. It wasn't hard to do. GM was a big company, so some part of it was always doing well. Besides, the vast majority of GM employees were smart, hardworking, well-meaning people of whom it was difficult to think ill. The atmosphere was always upbeat. Never— including today—was there a suggestion that better times were not just around the corner. The man who was poised to become chairman and CEO in 1981 exemplified GM's can-do attitude. He had the right instincts but the wrong ideas, and he implemented them so poorly that he caused more damage to the company than any other man. You can draw a straight line from the tenure of Roger Bonham Smith from 1981 to 1990 all the way to the bankruptcy of 2009.

CHAPTER 4

Insecure Colossus: The Roger Smith Era

Perhaps it was the influence of growing up in the 1950s with *Time* magazine in the house, or reading articles and books about Henry Luce and his influence, or living in Fairfield County with its overpopulation of publishing and advertising executives. Whatever the reason, I always felt that working at the Time & Life Building in New York City would be a career pinnacle, representing glamour, sophistication, and journalistic achievement.

I got there, but it wasn't easy and required a long and circuitous journey. While in Grand Rapids, I had leveraged the accidental presidency of Gerald Ford into a job as a stringer for *People* magazine, a Time Inc. publication, which was then concerned far less with celebrities and more with average individuals who did extraordinary things. Writing about Ford's friends, classmates, and acquaintances from his hometown, I landed half a dozen stories in the magazine and got my name listed on the masthead. When I moved to Detroit in 1977, I started picking up stringer assignments from *Time* as well as *People* and began lobbying for a staff job.

I got a break in 1979 when an opening developed in the "Economy & Business" section for somebody who knew the auto business. The next time that legendary *Time* editor Marshall Loeb came to Detroit, I arranged to meet with him. Loeb arrived on a Sunday night, the very day that two of my bylined stories wound up on the front page of the *Free Press*—the only time that ever happened. It must have been an omen. Like *Time* founder Henry Luce, Marshall liked to test job applicants by riding around town with them and quizzing them about local landmarks. I didn't ace the test, but Marshall and I seemed to hit it off over lunch at the historic London Chop House in downtown Detroit, and he offered me a job a couple of months later.

(Within weeks of my arriving at *Time*, Marshall would depart to become managing editor of another Time Inc. publication, *Money*, but our paths would cross again. In early 1986, I moved to *Fortune*, and Marshall showed up several months later and ran the magazine for eight successful years. A Midwesterner by birth, Marshall had an enduring interest in the auto industry and prodded me to write dozens of stories. Some, especially those on GM, were critical and endangered some of *Fortune*'s advertising but Marshall was steadfast in his support. He retired from Time Inc. in 1994 but continued to work at other journalistic enterprises for more than a decade—and continued to mentor me and many other journalists whose careers he had promoted over the years.)

So in 1980, I left Detroit for New York and a job writing for the business pages of *Time* magazine. The peak of the newsmagazine era had passed, but *Time* was still a huge journalistic enterprise, with correspondents around the world, an internal administrative apparatus that would rival the U.S. Army, and a circulation of four million. National politics and cultural coverage were *Time*'s pillars, but the energy crisis, inflation, and globalization were all making its reporting of business and the economy more sophisticated, and with Loeb's energetic leadership, we were allocated five or six pages of prime editorial real estate every week.

Under the newsmagazine system, I depended on our correspondents in the field to report on the industry; I wrote articles based on their files. The magazine closed on Friday nights, and I frequently worked past midnight, fueled by hot dinners provided by the commissary and adult beverages served from the drinks cart. In that pre-computer era, editorial changes were made by pencil, and last-minute trims, called "greens," were indicated by a pencil with green lead. As night turned into day on Saturday, we sat around waiting for top editors to look over our copy, frequently wondering if the copy had been lost or the editor had forgotten to come back after dinner.

While living and working in Manhattan, I would still go back to Detroit for special assignments and to visit my in-laws. I had met Mary, my wife-to-be, while working at the *Free Press*, and she had moved to New York eighteen months ahead of me for a promising job in corporate communications. We married in 1983. She had deep roots in Detroit and strong connections with GM—both her father and her sister worked for the company—but the auto industry was rarely a topic for our dinner-table conversation.

By then GM had found a chief executive who actually understood that the company was troubled and was willing to try almost anything to fix it. Roger Smith was part of the same finance fraternity as Donner, Gerstenberg, and Murphy, but he was far less inclined to accept the status quo. Smith understood that making decisions in the same laborious way that GM had fifty years earlier wouldn't cut it any longer because the company was falling behind competitors, especially Toyota. He was full of innovative ideas for upending business as usual—but some were badly thought out, others were poorly implemented, and all were expensive. Under Smith, GM lost more ground more quickly than under all his predecessors put together.

Smith's enduring battle was against the company's bureaucracy, the "frozen middle," he liked to call it. The conditions under which GM had prospered—a stable economy and an oligopoly controlled by three companies—were disappearing, and GM wasn't adapting to a faster-paced environment. It was beginning to resemble a corrupt government in which the bureaucrats ran the departments to suit their own needs rather than those of the voters. Once an industry leader, GM wasn't on the cutting edge of anything.

Smith's theory seemed to be that if he introduced enough irritants into the system, he would shake things up and produce positive results. Things DID get shaken up, but GM never got more efficient. Smith loved the grand gesture, the bold stroke that would push GM ahead, but he wasn't much for the actual details of implementation. Some of Smith's changes gummed up the works. Others proved to be distractions. Indefatigable and combative to the end, Smith never acknowledged that he had made any mistakes. It wasn't his leadership, he argued; he had been foiled by the frozen middle. Near the end of his tenure in 1989, he complained to *Fortune*'s Colin Leinster: "There we were, charging up the hill right on schedule, and I looked behind me and saw that many people were still at the bottom, trying to decide whether to come along."

Smith's general obliviousness reflected his isolation from the world outside Detroit. To polish GM's image along with his own

legacy, he ordered up a twenty-million-dollar public relations ex-
travaganza in 1988 to showcase GM's capabilities. The company
had suffered a number of setbacks, and Smith thought that display-
ing new models and concept cars as part of a musical revue would
boost GM's public standing. It was an idea straight out of the 1950s,
but Smith was unstoppable. The show, called "Teamwork and
Technology for Today and Tomorrow," was staged in the ballroom
of the Waldorf-Astoria Hotel in New York City.

I watched from the audience at the grand opening as Smith
fumbled his big moment. In an exchange with reporters, Smith
got a question from John White of the *Boston Globe* reflecting a
concern over rising consumer prices. "How come," White wanted
to know, "Chrysler can put a six-passenger car on the road for
$7,000 and you can't?" Replied Smith: "I think that our best com-
petition in General Motors against that car happens to be a two-
year-old Buick that you can get down at your dealer."

"A used car, sir?"

"Yes," insisted Smith. "There is a great value in it." The audience at the Waldorf was dumbstruck, and the automotive world
was buzzing for days. Smith's thoughtless remark, perfectly reflective of GM's arrogance and insularity, had erased any positive im-
pressions from "Teamwork and Technology." The notion that a
used GM car was better than anybody else's new model was laughable to everyone except Smith.

I had first met Smith in the 1970s when he was still an executive vice president of finance. He was already known for being easy
to caricature because of his high, squeaky voice and jittery man-
nerisms. Looking at his career, all of it spent at GM in North
America, he appeared to be just another successful corporate ap-

paratchik, a high-ranking bean counter. Any signs of the organizational iconoclast to come were invisible. When I interviewed Smith, he was approachable and agreeable. I was still learning a lot about the business, and he was patient with my uninformed questions. He was persistent, though. Instead of laughing away my misstatements, he never hesitated to contradict me if he thought I was wrong, and would keep at it until I changed the subject. I never found him to be mean or arrogant, though the people who worked for him did. They considered him a petty tyrant, demanding, and intolerant of dissenting ideas.

Smith knew that GM had big problems. The company was too inward-looking, too provincial, and too leaden. Billy Durant's assemblage of companies wasn't working efficiently enough to take advantage of its supposed economies of scale. According to GM's internal history, "In the 1980s, it was becoming painfully clear to more and more GM leaders that Sloan's organizational structure and the culture of independent and uncommon parts and processes had outlived their day. There had been some progress in adapting the structure and culture to a changing environment, but it was piecemeal and evolutionary; too little, too late."

The second oil crisis was about to send the company into a tailspin, as drivers fled—albeit temporarily—to smaller, more fuel-efficient import cars. GM had already downsized its large cars and brought out its first line of front-wheel-drive small cars, but it was still struggling to get them out of the factory. My first cover story for *Time*, dated September 8, 1980, quoted Smith, then an executive vice president, as likening the company to a hockey team in the midst of a line change. As soon as all the players are on the ice, he was certain, GM would be competitive again. It was an excuse

I would hear again and again from GM: "We're not doing so well right now, but wait until you see the new models we have coming next year."

As often as not, the market ignored the new GM models when they did arrive. Undoubtedly the most famous *Fortune* automobile cover appeared on the issue dated August 22, 1983. It featured four GM cars—a Chevrolet, an Oldsmobile, a Buick, and a Pontiac— photographed from above on a grass-green background. The angle of the photograph made the hoods, trunks, and roofs of the cars their most prominent feature, and since the metal stampings were nearly identical, the cars looked identical, too. They became known as the "lookalike cars," and they created a sensation be- cause they graphically illustrated a problem that bedeviled GM: how to maintain distinctions among the different brands when economies of scale dictated that they were all selling versions of essentially the same car. Why would someone need to move up the Sloan ladder from Chevrolet to Buick if the two cars were identical in everything except the brand on the trunk?

In terms of sheer damage to the company, nothing approached the reorganization Smith ordered in 1984. The problem he was trying to solve—an archaic operating structure—was real, but his solution and, more important, his implementation were so flawed that the company was tied up for eighteen months. New product programs languished because GM couldn't get anything done for a year and a half, and its market share slide accelerated, never to recover.

The reorganization was an attempt to eliminate a long-stand- ing problem. By the 1980s, GM's auto-making operation had barely evolved for sixty years. Car bodies were assembled by a sepa-

rate organization called Fisher Body. Then the bodies were trucked
to assembly plants, where the engines and running gear were installed by yet another organization, General Motors Assembly Division. If the marketing divisions wanted changes made, they had
to negotiate with one group or the other and then pay for the
changes on a cost-plus basis. It was expensive, inefficient, and hard
to manage. Both Fisher and GMAD maintained their own bu-
reaucracies and fiercely guarded their prerogatives. One longtime
Fisher Body manager described its operation as basically a black
box so separated from the rest of the company that a complex car
body would carry just a single part number when it was shipped
to GM.

Early in the 1980s, Smith made it his immediate priority to
shift the entire manufacturing system from body-on-frame to modern integrated structures. It was a needed change. Vehicle weight
had to be reduced, GM was moving to front-wheel-drive cars, and
customers wanted more interior space. The changeover made the
separate Fisher Body and GM Assembly Division structures re-
dundant. No longer would it make sense to have one unit building
bodies and another unit attaching them to a chassis. Integrated assembly meant that the entire car body would be fabricated and
welded in one place.

Smith's reorganization was intended to simplify GM's processes
by creating three centralized organizations to oversee all phases of
engineering and production: one for large cars, one for small cars,
and one for light trucks and commercial vehicles. But the company was too complex to carve up that neatly. Each of the two car
organizations ended up with responsibility for a mixed bag of small,

midsize, and large cars. Worse, they were organized differently and shared virtually no common processes, so there were few economies of scale.

It went downhill from there. According to GM's history, "In addition to tearing apart informal communication networks that really served as the glue, each of the new organizations created its own engineering structure and processes. With the reorg, duplication and complexity increased almost exponentially, and product lead times as well as quality suffered."

Instead of trimming its workforce by integrating Fisher and GMAD, GM had become so inefficient that it had to add people. In 1983, GM employed 691,000 people. By 1985, the number had climbed to 811,000. The hiring was especially massive at the "small car" group, Chevrolet-Pontiac-Canada. In 1985, CPC produced 3.5 million cars—roughly the same number as Toyota. But CPC employed 160,000 people, Toyota only 60,000.

The most visible casualty of the reorganization was the GM-10 program. Begun in 1982, it was designed to provide new midsize coupes, sedans, and station wagons for Chevy, Pontiac, Oldsmobile, and Buick. Instead of dividing the work among the four divisions, program boss Bob Dorn was supposed to gather resources from around the company for the design and engineering. But within GM's turf-conscious, cover-your-ass culture, cooperative endeavors were nearly impossible. Dorn couldn't get the help he needed, deadlines weren't met, and the budget quickly fractured. The station wagons were an early casualty and were eliminated, but it still took six years for the first models, the Buick Regal and Olds Cutlass Supreme, to arrive in dealerships. When they got there, they had been so long in arriving that they looked dated. At the time, Toyota was refreshing its product line every four years.

Worse, the GM-10 planners misread the market and delayed the development of four-door sedans, which were growing in popularity, in favor of two-door coupes, a segment that was shrinking. Conceded one GM executive: "It is fair to say that the market has shifted more to sedans than when we envisioned the program." Then, since Smith was trying to rein in costs, GM decided to stretch out the sedans' introduction, making them even tardier in reaching the market. In all, the cars cost seven billion dollars to develop and were so ineptly engineered and sold so poorly that GM lost two thousand dollars on each one. "I watched millions of dollars get pissed down the drain on the GM-10 program," Bill Hoglund told *Automotive News*. "The original GM-10 program probably turned out to be the worst program that GM ever did."

The reorganization became emblematic of the Roger Smith era: big idea, lousy execution, lasting consequences. As if it wasn't bad enough on its own terms, it so traumatized future CEOs that they never again attempted anything so radical. "One reorg per generation is enough" became the mantra, so Jack Smith and Rick Wagoner tried gradualism instead. It was a big mistake.

The rest of Smith's initiatives fared little better. In fact, you could argue that his was the most inept administration of an automaker since Henry Ford refused to replace the Model T until 1927 and thus forfeited Ford Motor's position as the industry leader. Wrote Monks and Minow: "Over the next decade, GM spent nearly $90 billion reforming itself. By most accounts, the money was all but wasted. GM lost market share throughout the 1980s and became a high-cost inefficient producer."

Always looking for a magical solution to GM's complex problems, Smith spent liberally on new technology. Through a joint
venture with a Japanese manufacturer, GM became the largest
maker of robots in the world, and Smith invested billions to auto-
mate GM's factories with the devices. Usually robots permit a car
company to produce several models in one factory. But GM, in an
effort to keep things simple and improve quality, configured its
plants to produce just one or two models—and thus ended up with
a system that, though more expensive, was no more efficient than
the one it replaced.

In fact, the more Smith spent, the less competitive GM became. At the beginning of Smith's tenure in 1983, according to
Monks and Minow, GM had the best operating margins in Detroit, two percentage points higher than either Ford or Chrysler. By
1985, the tables had turned, and those two companies were three
percentage points more efficient, despite all of GM's spending.
GM's sales increased 22 percent over that two-year period, but
earnings declined 35 percent. And whereas in 1980, GM could
produce a car for three hundred dollars less than Ford or Chrysler,
by 1986, GM was spending three hundred dollars more than Ford
or Chrysler.

All of the organizational churning took its toll on GM's sales
and marketing. In 1986, GM's market share took its biggest one-
year drop ever, falling nearly five points to 36.6 percent. It was an
astonishing performance at a time when a point of market share
represented sales of some 150,000 vehicles. Smith wanted GM to
develop cars more quickly, but as it rushed cars out, GM failed to
pay attention to quality. Most GM models through the 1980s
weren't as good as the vehicles they replaced. Because of union

rules that limited layoffs, sales fell faster than GM could reduce capacity. Slack demand, especially for the GM-10 cars, which were
built in dedicated factories, underlined GM's inflexibility and inability to adapt. GM still retained the production capacity to serve 50
percent of the market, but its share was sinking toward 35 percent.

Increasingly, my thinking on GM was being influenced by
analyst Maryann Keller. Keller combined a razor-sharp intelligence
with an absolute refusal to take anything at face value, as well as an
ability to see around corners and peer into culs-de-sac. She developed an extensive network of sources within the company, who
kept her up to date on the latest GM miscues, and she was consistently distrustful and always bearish — instincts that served her very
well. Another expert who spoke freely with me was David Cole of
the University of Michigan, the son of Corvair creator Ed Cole,
who knew GM and the rest of the industry inside and out. Cole
valued his connections to top executives and was too discrete to
gossip or reveal secrets. But at times, his remarks could be pene-
tratingly prescient. In 1990, I quoted him as saying, "The Big
Three are going to be hard pressed to manage the accelerating
change in the next few years." Those "next few years" would stretch
into two decades.

Even for someone as relentlessly upbeat as Roger Smith, the
cascading problems were leaving their mark. When I interviewed
him in the summer of 1987 for a *Fortune* feature called "Biggest
Bosses," he made a surprising admission. Smith's normally ruddy
face was covered with a red rash, a painless but disfiguring skin
problem that he attributed "99% to stress." When the magazine
came out, the disclosure knocked GM's stock down a few points,
according to the *Wall Street Journal*'s "Heard on the Street" col-

umn. If the relentlessly optimistic Smith was feeling stress, how was the rest of the company holding up?

A psychoanalyst would have a good time interpreting another remark Smith made to me for the same story. In response to a long-forgotten question, Smith said, "I am not really the horned monster that a lot of people assume. That's not me. I like people. Sure, I'm impatient. But I try to keep out of the daily running of the operations side of the business, not that it isn't temping to stick my nose in." That must have been his subconscious speaking. It brings to mind Richard Nixon's "I am not a crook" statement on Watergate. Horned monster or not, given the results Smith should have stuck his nose in a lot more often.

For all of the upheaval Smith produced, the bureaucracy was still winning. According to GM's history, "By the end of the 1980s, the policy committee and staff system originally devised for 'coordinated control' had itself become a complex bureaucracy. Even such relatively small decisions as names for new vehicle models and approvals for individual dealership franchises had to be approved at the corporate policy committee level rather than at the operational level. Committee staffs as well as the operating units found themselves spending more and more time on gathering more and more data to defend their own position within the company; time and effort that might otherwise have gone to improving products, efficiency, and service to the customer. But the 'GM Way' was the only way most leaders had ever dealt with problems, and it had always worked. With their careers nurtured in the GM structure, the search for answers was conducted within the structure itself. There was little sense of urgency for changing this culture and structure."

At the same time that Smith was trying to pinch pennies to fund his grandiose schemes, he displayed an unfortunate tendency to pad his own pocket. Worse, he was clumsy about it. Early in his tenure, GM signed a new contact with the UAW that stressed "shared sacrifice" to get through hard times. But when GM's proxy statement was published, it showed the company was considering a new bonus plan that would award five million shares to six hundred top executives, including of course, Smith. Years later, on his way out the door at age sixty-five, he tried to double his retirement pension to $1.2 million a year. It didn't play well once exposed, especially at a time when unionized GM workers were undergoing layoffs, and the increase was eventually dialed back.

Smith also used a sharp pencil to cover up GM's deteriorating financial performance. In "The Tasks Facing General Motors," in the March 13, 1989, issue of *Fortune*, I noted that a third of GM's "record" 1988 earnings could be attributed to bookkeeping changes. Among other things, the company lengthened the maximum period it used to depreciate plants from thirty-five years to forty-five, thus lessening the impact on reported earnings. Smith also rejiggered the projected returns for GM's pension fund, thereby availing himself of spare cash to help repair an increasingly distressed balance sheet.

Smith had a tendency to be argumentative and to deflect responsibility for mistakes—characteristics that wore thin after repeated miscues over eight years as CEO. In one of my last interviews with him, Smith conceded that he did not effectively communicate his goals for transforming GM's structure, technology, or management style or make sure they were met—core responsibilities CEO. Then he tried to sugarcoat his admission by hyping

Saturn, his grand effort to revolutionize the auto business. "The car will surprise you," he told me. "It will be different than anybody thinks it is going to be." Saturn was surprising and different, but it wasn't successful.

Smith's stormy relationship with Electronic Data Systems's Ross Perot highlighted two of the worst points of his character: his inability to accept criticism and his willingness to solve problems by throwing money at them.

After GM bought EDS in 1984, Perot became one of its biggest shareholders and won a seat on the board of directors. On arriving for his first meeting, he discovered he had been placed on the public policy committee, the least influential of any of the board committees. His relationship with GM went downhill from there. The entrepreneurial Perot found little to like at inefficient, bureaucratic GM and plenty to criticize. He wanted the board to become a genuine decision-making body, not a silent ratifying council that had been cowed into submission by the domineering Smith. Perot discovered that GM was so preoccupied with procedures as it bucked decisions up and down the organization chart that it failed to focus on results. He also noticed that Smith's massive capital spending program was doing little to solve the company's fundamental problems of quality and inefficiency. Accordingly, he was the only director who voted against the purchase of Hughes Aircraft, which Smith heralded as a high-tech diversification.

With his vividly colorful way of expressing himself and his willingness to use the media for a bully pulpit, Perot had no trouble finding an audience for his criticisms. When asked if GM's board was a mere rubber stamp, Perot replied: "Hell, no. We'd have to upgrade it to be a rubber stamp." His pithy observations found their way into public circulation with alacrity. A popular one: "Let's say you and I were both hopeless drunks. Step one is you have to admit it. But we haven't taken that step. Go to Detroit: Everybody who drives cars knows otherwise, but the guys running the place still think they are better than BMW, Mercedes, Toyota, Honda et cetera. The car capital of the world is Toyota City, not Detroit, yet Americans still daydream we are Number One."

Perot quickly became an irritant, so Smith did what had become second nature: he bought Perot out in a deal that had elements of both greenmail and a golden parachute. To get him to go away, GM offered Perot $61.90 for his GM shares that were then trading at $33—nearly double the market price. The total came to $742.8 million. Perot left the board at the end of 1986. That didn't stop him from tearing into GM and Smith at every available opportunity. *Fortune* gave him a platform in its February 1988 issue, and Perot responded with gusto, laying out a thirteen-point plan to reform GM. It included some commonsense provisions—use money like a scalpel, not a bulldozer; make sure that people can no longer get promoted simply by keeping their noses clean—and some more incendiary ones—eliminate heated executive garages; close the fourteenth floor in the GM building and send the executives out to the field; sublet the directors' boardroom in New York.

Smith was given space in the same issue to rebut Perot and, not surprisingly, saw things differently. As to whether GM was so bureaucratic that managers couldn't make decisions, Smith said, "We make decisions every minute of the day." Some of Smith's rejoinders were scarcely credible. On handling customer complaints,

Smith said, "I often pick up the phone and call customers. Everybody here does that—that's how you learn what customers are thinking." As to whether management was scandalized when Perot suggested giving up the boardroom floor in New York, "Ross Perot never suggested that to me or anyone else I know." Concluded Smith: "He is more impatient than anyone else in the world. . . . We agree on the target, but not on how to get there." He made no mention of heated garages.

The fancy bookkeeping, the Perot episode, the falling market share—all were starting to erode the confidence of the board in Smith. So Smith decided to pack it with supporters. In 1988, Smith proposed to appoint three more GM officers as directors. That meant that insiders would represent 40 percent of the membership, giving Smith a near veto-proof plurality. But the board rebuffed him, and Smith had to withdraw the proposal. Nobody could remember a GM board doing that to a chairman.

Standing up to Smith was a prelude for the board's historic coup d'état four years later. When the upheaval came, Smith's less clever but no less stubborn successor, Bob Stempel, would bear the brunt of the attack. Some of the problems Stempel faced were his own making, others stemmed from Smith's tenure, and others had been brewing since the 1960s. The board's action was historic, but it was way late.

CHAPTER 5

Ford Speeds Up

With its air of prosperity, stability, and predictability, General Motors bore little resemblance to its more raffish crosstown rival, Ford. Controlled by the Ford family with its 40 percent share of the voting rights guaranteed by a special class of stock, the number two automaker was rife with palace intrigue. Executives jockeyed for favorable notice from whichever Ford was sitting as king. That of course made Ford much more fun for a journalist to cover. Sources with delicious secrets and fascinating gossip to pass on were far more abundant in Dearborn. The reason was simple: they had a lot more to talk about.

The sharp-elbowed company politics were embedded in Ford culture. Old Henry Ford and his thuggish subordinate Harry Bennett had installed a rule of fear in the 1920s and 1930s that never entirely vanished. Back then, there were stories about how an executive might discover he'd been fired when he saw that all the furniture in his office had been removed or that his office had disappeared altogether—its walls moved in such a way as to make it appear as if it had never existed. Even into the 1980s, executives worried about wiretaps and electronic listening devices that would allow their conversations to be overheard. Unlike at GM, it was rare for Ford executives to hang onto their jobs until retirement; almost everyone was vulnerable to being toppled. The Dearborn company became known as a place where tough guys win.

I would come up against Ford's bare-knuckle approach early in my career at *Fortune*. I was told that Ford lawyers questioned people who were believed to be sources for stories I had written, that company phone records were searched to find out who was calling me, and that, in one case, an executive was fired because he was suspected of being a source. I was fed false rumors to throw me off a critical story and once was warned that I would be followed by Ford operatives on a trip to Dearborn.

I didn't like the pressure, but no direct harm came to me—unlike the people suspected of being my sources, who answered the lawyers' questions and whose careers were affected. What it did mean was that reporting on Ford came with higher stakes—and produced vivid, visceral stories that just didn't exist at a company like GM. The best ones revealed collisions between the Ford family and the nonfamily executives who ran the company for them.

During my *Free Press* years from 1977 to 1980, Henry Ford II, grandson of company founder Henry Ford and the chairman and CEO, was Detroit royalty, the king of the city. His inherited position as proprietor of his family's company conveyed more status than the up-the-organization strivings of corporate suits at GM, who were nothing but employees. It didn't hurt that Hank the Deuce, as he was known, had flair and presence to spare, with his monogrammed shirts, fitted custom suits, and Italian loafers. Ford's lifestyle—Mediterranean cruises, homes in England and Palm Beach as well as in Grosse Pointe Farms—set him apart from everyone else in this mostly conservative town, as did his penchant for partying, occasionally with women to whom he wasn't married. It was also a more relaxed time. Bodyguards were rare back then. Ford was likely to show up, unaccompanied, at corporate functions, and I once bumped into him biking around Grosse Pointe after dinner with his wife.

Henry Ford II's imperial style led to impulsive decisions from which there was no appeal and to a continual shuffling of the executive deck chairs. He famously fired President Lee Iacocca in 1978 with the line, "I just don't like you."

When Ford retired as CEO in 1979, he installed Philip Caldwell, a starchy finance executive who drank nothing stronger than tea, as his successor, setting the stage for a memorable confrontation. Caldwell couldn't abide the less conventional behavior of the man Henry Ford chose to succeed him, Donald Petersen. Petersen, who launched some of Ford's most successful models, harbored an eccentric streak. The most visible sign of this was his extensive collection of football-sized crystals that he showed to office visitors. Less well known was his habit of clearing meetings from his calendar for several days a month so that he could use the time for thinking. His secretary designated them with a special pen, and they began to be called "magenta days." Petersen's eccentricities would prove grist for two of my most challenging and successful stories.

Petersen actively cultivated a New Age image. A year and a half after I arrived at *Fortune,* I published an interview with him in the August 3, 1987, issue. Petersen's habits and hobbies were more those of a college professor, I wrote. He was a member of Mensa, the high-IQ organization, and polished off a book every two weeks. This was unusual stuff for an auto executive.

Petersen's wife became a close friend of Henry Ford's third

wife, which didn't hurt Petersen's ascension through the executive ranks. But as CEO, Petersen was tone deaf when it came to other members of the Ford family, notably Henry's son, Edsel II, and Henry's nephew, Bill. Henry had famously declared that "there were no crown princes at Ford Motor Company," but nobody except Petersen took that seriously. He had appointed the two boys to the board of directors after Henry's death in 1987 but ignored them after that. His inability to take their ambitions seriously would have significant consequences for him and the company.

I suspected none of this when I approached the company in the fall of 1988 for its permission to write a story about the Ford family. *Fortune*'s Carol Loomis had produced a very successful takeout on the Rockefellers, and my story was supposed to proceed in a similar vein, exploring the lives of the third and fourth generations of the founding family. Initially, everything proceeded in a very conventional way. The company cleared the way for me to approach such family members as Henry's brother, William Clay, and sister, Josephine, as well as Edsel and Bill, for interviews and subsequent picture sessions.

As I proceeded, nothing seemed amiss. Except for a couple of young fourth-generation rebels who were sewing wild oats but were of no consequence to the company, the family was united in its determination to support Ford's professional management, hold on to their Ford Motor shares, and continue their control of the company. Near the end of my reporting, however, the quiet was broken in a follow-up phone call I made to Edsel. These days, it would be impossible for me to contact Edsel or anybody else of prominence at Ford without the call being intercepted and returned by the public relations department. But I got Edsel on the line, and without my asking, he revealed an unexpected split between the family and Petersen, who ran their company.

Did I realize, Edsel asked me, that Petersen had named him and his cousin Bill to the board of directors without putting them on any board committees? In other words, they had ceremonial positions but no real responsibilities, and as a result, neither spoke up during board meetings.

Edsel was angry about it, and so was Bill. After a series of follow-up interviews with Petersen, some conducted by my research associate David Morrow, we found we had broken a big story, which *Fortune*, as a fortnightly publication, rarely did.

The younger Fords wanted more representation on the board of directors, a bigger voice in strategic decisions, and larger roles in management. They felt thwarted by Petersen. Said Edsel: "I've made it clear on one or two occasions to Mr. Petersen that it does seem a bit odd to me that there are three classes of directors: inside, outside, and Billy and me." For his part, Petersen sounded as if he were in denial and, as the saying goes around Ford, had forgotten whose name is on the building. He said he felt that he must deal with shareholders on an equal basis, family or no family.

Identifying the source of Petersen's animus to the young Fords wasn't difficult. The son of a poor Minnesota farmer, Petersen was a self-made man, and the idea of advancement because of family ties was clearly anathema to him. Equally striking, though, was his inability to remember where his paycheck came from. Affable on most matters, Petersen froze at the mention of a Ford following him as CEO. "I'm not a caretaker for anybody," he said. "I admire the fact that (Edsel and Billy) are trying very hard to go as far as they can. But being a Ford does not give them a leg up. Selection to top management is based solely on merit.'"

In business journalism circles, the split between Petersen and the young Fords was big news. *Business Week* and *Newsweek* both published follow-up pieces citing *Fortune* as the source, and *Wall Street Journal* editor Norm Pearlstine (later to become editor in chief of Time Inc.) told associates that it was the first *Fortune* story he wished had appeared in the *Journal* first. A few days later, Edsel and Petersen appeared together at the Detroit auto show to shake hands in public and say nice things about each other in a widely reported event.

Despite the new focus on the role of the family in Ford's future, nobody could have predicted what happened next. Whatever his faults, Petersen had been associated with some of Ford's greatest successes. During his decade-long tenure as a top executive, first as president and then as CEO, Ford's U.S. market share had risen from 17 percent to 22 percent and the company bested General Motors in profits two years running, the first time that had happened since 1924. Petersen emphasized teamwork and long-term strategic thinking at the company—both laudable goals. And by directing development of the jelly bean–shaped, front-wheel-drive Taurus, he ignited Ford's product-led recovery in the mid-1980s.

So there was both shock and surprise when Petersen announced in November 1989 that he wanted to leave Ford eighteen months before his sixty-fifth birthday to, in his quaint phrase, "repot himself." There was no suggestion that Petersen's departure was anything less than voluntary. Until the February 11, 1991, issue of

Fortune, that is, when I reported that "several current and former members of Ford's board of directors and a high company executive contend that Petersen was forced out."

Just as a casual remark by Edsel Ford helped me uncover the family's disagreement with Petersen, a throwaway line by a Ford executive to the effect that "we got rid of Petersen" set me on a course of discovering what had actually happened to him. I eventually did, but only in the process of causing great pain to myself, my editors, and my Ford source. I also found myself caught in the crossfire between feuding factions of the company.

After I had done enough reporting to assure myself that Petersen had not left voluntarily, I presented my conclusions to Ford. I innocently expected the company to concede the matter but discovered that I had overplayed my hand. Ford stonewalled, and after making some informed guesses about who my sources were, the company went after them aggressively. After discovering records of a series of telephone calls between myself and an executive at the company, Ford lawyers questioned him for several hours. He told me what happened in a call from a pay phone. He was later fired, though his departure was described as a retirement.

My source was surprisingly gracious about the whole episode, claiming that he had been looking to leave the company all along, but I was crestfallen. I was also having my own problems with the story at the magazine. I had prepared a piece for the cover stating flatly that Petersen had been fired and had arranged an interview near the deadline with Ford's lead director, Clifton Wharton, who I expected would provide confirmation. In another burst of hubris over my big scoop, I invited managing editor Loeb to come along. But Wharton ran us around the block with double-talk and picked holes in my chronology of events. Back at the office, Loeb spiked my story and told me to do more reporting if I wanted my piece to run in the magazine.

Ford didn't let up. I was warned that I would be followed if I returned to Detroit, though I could never ascertain whether I actually was tailed when I did go back. To throw me farther off the story, an executive told me to pursue a particularly ugly rumor: whether Allan Gilmour, then the chief financial officer and a frequently mentioned candidate CEO, was gay. In fact, Gilmour was gay, as he revealed after his retirement (in an exclusive *Fortune* story). But I was determined to pin down the Petersen story and wasn't put off in my pursuit.

Having done more reporting, I was able to publish the Petersen story in a subsequent issue. It didn't run on the cover, and I presented less than an open-and-shut case, but I was able to raise plenty of intriguing points in "The Strange Demise of a Superstar CEO" that strongly suggested he had been pushed out. It turned out that the outside directors were increasingly unhappy with his performance and worried about how the company would be managed in the coming recession. Their dissatisfaction came to a head when they rejected Petersen's succession plans. According to a high-up company executive conversant with the board's doings: "He was told to leave and told he could call it anything he wanted."

It emerged that Petersen had turned off the board by believing his own press clippings and becoming remote and intolerant of criticism. One source close to the board called him "the man I know who comes closest to having ice water in his veins." Interviewd for the story, Petersen continued to contend that he had left voluntarily. He said he was tired of the CEO grind and wanted to give "my friend Red" Poling, the man who succeeded him, a chance to run the company. He also complained of health problems. Just as *Fortune* was going to press, he wrote the magazine to insist once again that it was his idea to retire early and that accounts to the contrary were absolute nonsense.

A key figure in Petersen's departure, it turned out, was Caldwell, the former CEO. The two men had feuded almost from the moment that Henry Ford II picked Petersen to be president. The bitterness continued after Petersen became CEO on Caldwell's retirement in 1985. Caldwell had made the tough decision to commit several billion dollars to build the dramatically styled Taurus and Sable, which proved to be hugely successful. But since the cars were launched after Caldwell retired, Petersen got the credit. When I interviewed Caldwell, he ripped into Petersen's record as CEO, though he refused to mention him by name. "The tenacity that has to be in the corner office wasn't there," Caldwell said. "The words were there, but words don't get it done. People should be making history, not reading it or talking about it. Instead of delegation, there was abdication."

There the story stood, until the publication in 1994 of an industry history called *Comeback,* by the *Wall Street Journal*'s Paul Ingrassia and Joe White, revealed more details of Petersen's departure. They reported that Ford's outside directors had tired of Petersen's imperious manner, as well as his handling of succession, and had decided that he needed to leave. Three directors individually delivered the news to the once high-flying CEO. In their notes, the authors graciously referenced my work, saying, "The authors verified Mr. Taylor's accounts, and obtained more detailed descriptions of the events that he first reported."

On its own, the story of Petersen's disaffection with the Ford family would be an interesting footnote to Ford history—except that, later in the decade, the story repeated itself. Another Ford CEO, Alex Trotman, who had differences with the Ford family, would air his dissatisfaction with the board of directors. Like Petersen, Trotman also would have to be reminded whose name was on the building.

CHAPTER 6

The Saturn Moonshot

Roger Smith called his big ideas "lulus," and Saturn was a lollapalooza. Frustrated and impatient with trying to cure GM's manufacturing, engineering, and marketing woes, Smith decided to start over again with a clean sheet of paper. So he created Saturn as a way to reinvent GM by doing everything differently. Smith tried to do it all at once. He tried to bypass GM's balkanized manufacturing system by combining all of Saturn's factory operations in one place. He tried to whitewash GM's sorry union relations by giving workers a piece of the action in exchange for more cooperation. He tried to solve GM's perennial small-car problem by creating a new division that would do nothing but make small cars. And he tried to create a cohesive and responsive dealer network by awarding dealers exclusive territories so that they wouldn't be forced to compete against one another.

As the famous ads would proclaim in the early 1990s, Saturn would be a different kind of car company. It really was a noble idea that had tremendous appeal. As GM vice chairman Bob Lutz said much later, the Saturn experiment was an attempt to answer the question, "Why can't we have it both ways? Let's have wonderful dealers and consumers who are enthusiastic about the product."

And parts of the original concept proved durable. Saturn did go on to set new standards for satisfied buyers and to form remarkably strong bonds with its customers. "The Saturn experience," which started with the dealer sale and ran through the life of the car, became the talk of the industry.

But even with a clean sheet and a blank check, Smith couldn't produce a winner. In its two decades of operation, Saturn built a gigantic new factory, introduced several all-new models, conducted massive ad campaigns, and consumed billions of dollars of GM's money. It was all in vain. The notion that a tiny independent American company such as Saturn could make low-margin small cars and sell them profitably proved totally unworkable. The Saturn cars weren't good enough, and GM couldn't charge enough for them. Meanwhile, competition from Japan and, later, Korea proved much tougher than anyone expected. Exactly twenty years after Saturn opened for business, GM put it up for sale to the highest bidder as part of its bankruptcy proceedings. When no buyers were found, GM closed it, orphaning hundreds of thousands of Saturn customers. By then, Roger Smith's concept of a new way of making and marketing cars was already dead.

As the biggest new idea out of Detroit since the Mustang, Saturn caused a sensation from the day of its announcement in 1985. Every byte of information that dribbled out was seized on by a waiting world. All of this proved to be irresistible for journalists. Always suckers for a prepackaged story line, they eagerly reported every stage in Saturn's development, as each decision point became an occasion for a giant media guessing game: What would the new division be named? What would the new car look like? Who would do the advertising? Finding a site for Saturn's assembly plant turned into the biggest nationwide search since David O. Selznick sought an actress to play Scarlett O'Hara in *Gone with the Wind*. With so much inherent drama to contend with, reporters put aside their normal skepticism. Quibbling would have seemed unpatriotic, since Smith was embarked on nothing less than an attempt to save the U.S. auto industry.

Parts of Saturn were genuinely innovative. Saturn dealers were encouraged to sell cars for a fixed price, thus eliminating the haggling that many customers found repugnant. The inaugural advertising was a hit. The "different kind of car, different kind of company" campaign, created by the Hal Riney agency, cleverly focused more on the rural assembly plant in Tennessee and the down-home people who worked in it than on the vehicles themselves. The intent of the ads, which never mentioned GM, was to attract import buyers who otherwise wouldn't shop for a GM car. Most of the TV spots were unabashedly corny. One featured a ten-year-old boy and his dog who were uprooted from their Midwest home when the boy's father moved to work for Saturn and the family began a new life in friendly Spring Hill. But they created attention and a favorable, homey image for Saturn.

Smith's initial plan for Saturn to leapfrog the Japanese with new technology didn't remain intact for long. As GM's financial fortunes waxed, Saturn's initial budget was cut from five billion dollars to less than four billion, and the emphasis shifted from exploring the leading edge in manufacturing and engineering to building a high-volume car that would capture customers interested in smaller imports.

Saturn's managers quickly learned that they were embarked on a perilous mission because they began deflating some of the more inflated expectations that had been erected for Saturn. The assembly plant was nothing special, and neither was the car. There would be no "lights out" factories with automated machinery replacing workers, no fifty-mile-per-gallon engines. Inevitably, the price of a Saturn car crept up, from six thousand dollars at the time of Smith's announcement to ten thousand to twelve thousand, far more than the price for a comparable Japanese subcompact. "Saturn is no longer an experiment," declared general manager Skip Le Fauve at one point. "We're not a laboratory. We're not a social program. We're a business." It was something Smith should have emphasized from the beginning, but the message got lost in all the hype.

Smith's starry-eyed vision of the future caused all but the most hardened cynics to overlook the obvious flaws in Saturn's business model. Even with its reduced start-up costs, Saturn was burdened by so much overhead that, given the narrow margins available on small cars, it could never be profitable. Though GM was burdened by overcapacity, nobody asked why it was building another billion-dollar assembly plant. Nor did they ask why Saturn would sacrifice one of GM's genuine advantages, economies of scale, by trying to do everything on its own. Instead of sharing parts with other divisions, it would be sourcing them by itself and paying higher prices. Nor would the dealers be in a position to make much money; the product line was limited—only a coupe, sedan, and wagon at first—and they were restricted from selling other brands.

Before Saturn opened for business in 1990, I was one of a small group of journalists given an opportunity to look at and drive the first Saturn cars. Vehicle evaluation was never my strong point—I'm not an engineer or even a real car enthusiast, though I do pay attention to what engineers and enthusiasts are saying—but I quickly determined that what GM had created with its clean sheet of paper was unexceptional.

The cars looked like smaller versions of Oldsmobile's Cutlass Supreme, one of the GM-10 cars that was having a tough time in the market, and were equipped with run-of-the-mill engines and transmissions. Saturn's big idea when it came to engineering was plastic body panels that were dent-resistant, but they turned out to be expensive, heavy, and hard to work with. An early idea that owners would periodically unbolt the colored body panels from their frames and exchange them for different ones was quickly abandoned as impractical. Characteristically, engineers figured out the plastic bodies were a bad idea long before they were abandoned, but Saturn stayed with them because they thought they were important to its brand identity. They weren't. Once they were replaced by lighter and cheaper steel ones, nobody missed them.

A by-now widely unpopular Smith drove the first Saturn car off the assembly line in 1990 days before he retired and then left it to his successors to create a viable strategy. Just two years later, Saturn's troubles began in earnest when Smith's handpicked successor, Robert Stempel, was pushed from office. That left Saturn without a friend at the top of the company. Other GM divisions, particularly Chevy, were jealous of Saturn's special treatment and successfully battled it for scarce capital. Saturn executives felt as if they had been disinherited. "The genius of Roger's plan was he put us off to the side," Don Hudler, a Saturn veteran who served as president from 1995 to 1998 and eventually bought six Saturn dealerships, told me. "That cost us a lot because a lot of people in GM hated us for that. It is like being a very young child born into a wealthy family. We were getting some of their money." Not enough, as it turned out. Until the very end, Saturn was starved for capital.

Saturn sales peaked in 1994 at 286,000 units. Stempel's successor, Jack Smith, couldn't make up his mind what Saturn needed to be, so product decisions were delayed. And when new models did arrive, they were invariably disappointing, distinguished neither by design nor by performance. Gas prices stayed low in the 1990s, dampening demand for small cars, and Saturn was late in cashing in on the sport-utility vehicle boom. Saturn got the "different" part; it just never figured out how to be better.

While Saturn was struggling in the United States, its executives inexplicably decided that the time was right for an attack on the most intransigent small-car market with the pickiest customers on earth: Japan. So in 1997 it began building right-hand-drive Saturns and shipping them to new stand-alone dealerships in Tokyo and other cities. Saturn aimed to sell three to four thousand cars its first year, but Japanese consumers, who had access to the best small cars in the world, bought only fourteen hundred during the first sixteen months. I went over to have a look during a trip to the Tokyo Motor Show, and the dealerships were empty. Saturn executives talked bravely about staying in Japan for the long haul after steep losses, but they abandoned the effort in 2000.

Meanwhile, GM sacrificed another division, Oldsmobile, to keep Saturn alive. It couldn't afford to support all its brands, so in December 2000 it killed Olds, which had once sold more than a million cars per year. Should GM have let Saturn die instead? "That's a moot point and is best suited to a stimulating but fruitless intellectual debate," said Bob Lutz. He argued that Olds overlapped with other divisions while Saturn got a different kind of buyer who wouldn't ordinarily shop GM, "and that's of huge strategic importance." Longtime industry observer Dave Cole was more direct. "Would they ever do a Saturn again in the current situation?" asked Cole, head of the Center for Automotive Research in Ann Arbor. "No, I don't think so."

To boost customer appeal, Saturn began to expand its product line with larger cars. The first midsized Saturn, the L200, was introduced in1999. Anonymously styled and subpar in almost every way, it was discontinued prematurely in 2005. With losses mounting, GM had to figure out how to run Saturn on the cheap, in effect destroying Roger Smith's original concept in order to save it. Earlier, GM had taken away Saturn's special independent status and made it into another division like Pontiac and Buick, with the same centralized engineering and manufacturing. It also dissolved the special contract with the United Auto Workers. Now, unlike the original models that were designed by Saturn stylists, developed by Saturn engineers, and built in a dedicated Saturn plant, the new vehicles would come from GM's development system and would be built in GM factories alongside other brands. The savings that came along with that would permit additional new models.

Saturn would get one more chance at survival, as I would later report in *Fortune*. A small drama played out involving a determined young woman, surprising support from the top of the company, and additional funds and enthusiasm. Had the effort worked, it would have been a fairy-tale ending. But it came too late: competition was too strong and GM's reputation too weak.

The would-be Cinderella behind the revitalized Saturn was Jill Lajdziak, who had been with Saturn since the beginning and had risen to become its top sales and marketing executive in 1999. The energetic Lajdziak (pronounced LAY-jack) smartly believed that Saturn's original concept had reached a dead end. For Saturn to survive, she believed it needed to boost volume and develop additional products in higher-profit segments by adapting existing GM designs.

Lajdziak got a chance to put her ideas into action after Lutz, her Prince Charming, arrived at GM in 2001. At a dinner after the January 2002 Detroit auto show, Lutz asked Lajdziak and other division heads for ideas on how to improve their performance. Lajdziak sent back a multipage letter outlining new product and marketing ideas. She had nothing to lose because GM had completely ignored Saturn in its future product planning. Saturn was expected to limp along indefinitely with its lineup of three outdated vehicles.

Lajdziak won Lutz over, and he assigned Ed Welburn, GM's head of advanced design, to create new styling themes for the brand. The diplomatic Welburn, who had served a two-year stint at Saturn in the 1990s, would become GM's chief designer in 2004. But his first effort didn't "reach far enough," Lajdziak decided, and Lutz backed her up. "Jill made it clear that it wasn't the right vehicle for the brand," Welburn said. Lajdziak wanted something more daring—something that would push this perennial design laggard to the forefront. So Welburn solicited proposals from seven of GM's eleven global design studios, relying especially heavily on Opel in Russelsheim, Germany, where he had worked in the late 1990s. Some Opel designers moved to Detroit to work on Saturn.

GM's board of directors was briefed on the new model program as it progressed, and the board approved the expenditure of another three billion dollars on Saturn through 2007. The way GM saw it, there was nothing wrong with Saturn that a few new models wouldn't cure. "We're investing in Saturn's future because the inherent health of the brand is quite good," said Lutz. "It just needs a bigger, more exciting product portfolio." The Saturn name was arguably stronger than some others at GM. Saturn regularly ranked alongside Lexus and Infiniti in terms of customer satisfaction. And Saturn owners were extremely loyal to their dealers, who requited the love with a thirty-day return policy, easy service appointments, and other displays of affection.

Then there were those conquest sales. Because of its positioning and marketing, Saturn was a wedge into a world of car buyers GM couldn't otherwise reach. According to the company's research, 70 percent of Saturn buyers didn't consider buying another GM car. Saturn, they liked to say, was a "channel to a larger ocean."

The main victim of the Lajdziak's new Saturn strategy was distinctiveness. To save money, GM reverted to badge engineering. The 2005 Saturn Relay "sport van" was being marketed under different names by three other divisions: Chevy, Pontiac, and Buick. Saturn's convertible two-seater, named Sky, was built from the same architecture as Pontiac's Solstice. Analysts wondered whether selling a hot car like Sky to sensible Saturn buyers wasn't akin to marketing tournament snowboards to grandmothers. Lutz countered by saying that tapping into GM's global resources was "exactly what [would] deliver the variety of product Saturn needs."

But Saturn's moment had passed. Foreign competition, particularly from Koreans Hyundai and Kia, which hadn't even entered the market when Smith conceived Saturn, was stronger than ever, and Saturn's offerings had little besides looks to distinguish themselves. The addition of new models based on Opel designs didn't help and were very expensive to build. Saturn executives had said they expected to boost volume from the 215,000 units for 2004 to 400,000 in 2007. They never came close. Saturn sold only 240,091 cars in 2007 and then 188,004 in 2008. With GM declaring bankruptcy, sales were down another 58 percent in 2009. The plant in Spring Hill, Tennessee, about which Hal Riney had rhapsodized, stopped making Saturn cars in 2007 and was scheduled to be closed.

When GM put Saturn up for "strategic review" in 2009, it attracted a surprising amount of interest from outsiders. At one point, some sixteen interested parties were said to be considering taking Saturn off GM's hands. Entrepreneur Roger Penske became the last bidder standing. Penske, who ran a chain of car dealerships during the week and oversaw race car teams on weekends, was mostly interested in the distribution channel offered by Saturn dealers. He planned to keep selling three of GM's Saturn models for a couple of years and then shift over to selling small cars made in Korea by Renault. Opinions were widely divided over whether his strategy would succeed. Few distributors like Penske were able to manage product development and manufacturing as well as sales.

In the end, Penske couldn't get Renault or any other manufacturer to guarantee a supply of cars. So Roger Smith's Saturn dream died. Except for one or two years in the 1990s, Saturn never made an operating profit, and overall, I estimate GM invested ten to fifteen billion dollars in it with no return. At the same time that Saturn was starting up, Toyota launched its upscale Lexus division with two cars. There was a lot more skepticism about Toyota's ability to create a luxury brand than there was about Saturn, but Lexus went on to become the best-selling luxury car in the United States and earned a reputation as one of the most reliable cars ever built. But then, Toyota has a history of exceeding expectations. GM's reputation is quite different.

CHAPTER 7

Lee Iacocca, Blemishes and All

Looking on from offstage while GM struggled to reinvent itself was another automaker and its chief executive: Chrysler chairman and CEO Lee Iacocca. With his swagger, deft phrasemaking, and undisguised appreciation of the good life, Iacocca radiated more charisma on his own than a room full of GM suits. He was a magnet for editors because he usually said outrageous and unpredictable things—and because he sold magazines. Before Apple's Steve Jobs became *Fortune's* most reliable newsstand seller, Iacocca was one of its favorite cover subjects. Even after he left Chrysler, he became that rare retired executive who continued to appear in the magazine, landing on the cover twice.

Having covered Iacocca in Detroit and written about him at *Time,* I was the logical candidate for the Iacocca beat at *Fortune.* I guarded it protectively and enjoyed every minute spent with my subject. Being welcomed by the man at his Chrysler office in Highland Park, the marble-walled Chrysler boardroom in Manhattan, or his homes in Palm Springs and Bel Air was like being admitted to a special club in which Iacocca controlled the membership.

Once you were in, you were a friend for life and forgiven all but the most egregious failings.

Iacocca, of course, was that rare auto man who transcended the industry and became a celebrity outside it, with his TV commercials, books and speeches, and flirtation with presidential politics. By spending time with him, you got a view of a wider world beyond Detroit and a glimpse of Iacocca cronies, among them Frank Sinatra, George Steinbrenner, and Gianni Agnelli. You also got to peek into a very unusual psyche. Iacocca unself-consciously exposed his feelings to anyone who was willing to listen. He did so in a mostly appealing way that made you a coconspirator in whatever was on his mind.

Because of Iacocca's immense drawing power, along with his occasional tendency to open his mouth before engaging his brain, *Fortune* ran more verbatim interviews with him than any other CEO, with the possible exception of Warren Buffett. Iacocca loved to talk, ranged widely in his references, and told wonderful stories. All I had to do was turn on my tape recorder, suggest a line of inquiry, and then figuratively put my feet up and listen.

As smart and successful as he was, Iacocca was an insecure man who wore his neuroses on his sleeve. Despite his immense popularity, he didn't like speaking in public. He got nervous when appearing before large groups and fussed endlessly over his speeches. In his office, he seemed helpless when he wasn't surrounded by his factotums; at home, his wife, a personal assistant, or a housekeeper stood by to look after him. Always aware of his Italian heritage, he yearned to be accepted by what he considered the upper crust. For years after Henry Ford II fired him in 1978, Iacocca would talk about Ford as if the incident had happened only the day before. I came to believe that aside from the professional hurt, he was most upset because he could no longer maintain the illusion of being Hank the Deuce's social equal.

Iacocca was famous for his searing temper and for frequently blistering subordinates. I never myself was exposed to an Iacocca blowup, though a letter or two I received after a story had to be handled with tongs and asbestos gloves. But he didn't appear to hold a grudge, and once the storm blew over, the seas were calm again.

My first encounter with the man whom I would later refer to as "Detroit's living legend" was inauspicious. After being fired by Ford in 1978, Iacocca had remained on the payroll for a few weeks to complete an employment agreement and fulfill a pension requirement, and he had been assigned ground-floor office space in a Ford parts warehouse on the outskirts of Detroit, miles from company headquarters. The *Free Press*, where I worked, had gotten a tip about his whereabouts, and since he had been out of public view since his dismissal, I was sent out with a photographer to try to interview him.

Somehow managing to talk our way past the parking lot guard, the photographer and I were lurking in the warehouse lobby when Iacocca breezed in after lunch. I approached him with questions, but, never breaking his stride, he brushed me aside, walked through the doors, and proceeded down a linoleum-covered hallway to his modest office. The total journalistic content of the incident was an account of my pursuit, his response ("I can't see you now"), and a picture of his Continental Mark V with a thousand-dollar carriage roof option parked in a no-parking zone in front of the warehouse. Still, it was good enough to land on page 3 of the next day's *Free*

Press and earn a mention by Walter Cronkite on the *CBS Evening News* that night.

A couple of years later, Iacocca became a hero when he arranged a $1.5 billion government loan to keep Chrysler out of bankruptcy and then went on television to help sell the company's new small K-cars. He was one of the first CEOs to shill for his own products in person, and he was good at it, putting real feeling into his tagline, "If you can find a better car, buy it." I wrote a cover story about him for *Time* in 1983, and Iacocca-mania erupted shortly thereafter when his book took off and he flirted with the prospect of running for president.

Still, as it did for all its life as an independent company, Chrysler led a precarious existence, swinging between prosperity and poverty. As the 1980s sales boom began to wind down, Chrysler was in trouble again. Iacocca was never much interested in the nitty-gritty of daily operations. He tended to coast when times were good and became distracted by grandiose schemes to boost the share price, which would benefit him as well as other stockholders. To convince Wall Street that the company needed to be valued as a growth company and not a stodgy auto manufacturer, he reorganized Chrysler as a holding company and established an aerospace division by acquiring corporate jet maker Gulfstream and a defense electronics company. Neither amounted to much, but Iacocca made a smarter buy when he doubled down on the auto business by buying tiny American Motors in 1987. Iacocca discarded the Renaults AMC was selling but invested in its Jeep brand and made the four-door Jeep Cherokee the first widely popular SUV.

Unlike most executives, Iacocca was comfortable enough in

his position to riff on the shortcomings of competitors. In a *Fortune* cover story for the August 29, 1988, issue, headlined "The Lion in Winter," he analyzed GM's market-share collapse under Roger Smith. Iacocca was philosophical: Chrysler had gotten over its bad times, and now GM was enduring them, and he was shocked by how far it had fallen. Iacocca didn't blame Smith or the acquisitions of Hughes and EDS (although he thought the Hughes acquisition was "crazy") but attributed its share loss to the fact that the imports' gains had to come from somewhere and GM had the most to lose. Unlike most in the industry, Iacocca didn't think GM would come back. Even though it had a 37 percent market share, he figured it would never return to 40 percent, any more than imports were going to drop again to under 30 percent.

Then Iacocca began to let his feelings show, saying he felt sorry for Smith because he (Iacocca) had been through tough times, too, when Chrysler went begging for a government loan. He thought history would be kinder to Smith than the media had been. GM's problem weren't that its cars looked alike because they always had, in Iacocca's view. The problem was that its costs were too high because it had never adapted to a lower level of sales volume.

His most interesting comment was his explanation of why he hadn't gone to work at GM after he was fired at Ford: "They would have said to me, 'We can't use you because you haven't had at least 40 years at GM, gone to General Motors Institute, come up through the ranks, and stepped on every rung on the ladder. We never go to the outside for executives because that's an admission that we didn't build our people right.'" That explanation could serve today as the key reason why GM stumbled into bankruptcy in 2009.

By 1990, Chrysler was getting deeper in financial trouble and closer to bankruptcy again. Iacocca had allowed important car lines to wither, seen his pet venture to build the thirty-three-thousand-dollar TC convertible with Maserati collapse in a two-hundred-million-dollar fiasco, and been distracted by his billion-dollar diversification scheme. But that didn't stop him from sitting for another interview with *Fortune,* or *Fortune* from publishing it. As usual, it was unique. After all, how often do you hear a chief executive apologize for the poor quality of the products he sold? "From 1980 to 1985 the products we were shipping weren't as good as they should have been," said Iacocca with his usual disarming candor. "I'm not saying we were shipping crap, but little by little we began to lose our position."

Nobody enjoyed a crisis as much as Iacocca, and he was having so much fun at Chrysler, despite its problems, that he didn't want to leave as he approached retirement age. His intransigence caused succession issues. His longtime number two and heir presumptive, Gerald Greenwald, had gone off to lead an ultimately unsuccessful union buyout of United Airlines, but that did little to ease the backlog of potential CEOs still sitting on Chrysler's bench, beginning with product expert Bob Lutz.

As recently as January 1990, Iacocca had insisted he wanted out of day-to-day operations by December 1991, after he turned sixty-seven and his contract expired. But at Chrysler's annual meeting in May 1990, he hinted that he might stay on for another year—or longer. Then, shortly after Greenwald's departure, he announced that he definitely would remain past 1991, though he didn't say for how long. "Right now there's a battle raging," said Iacocca, "and I'm not going to leave my troops in the field."

By then, his troops probably needed a new general. Looking back, it is extraordinary how many of Chrysler's problems from that day, just like GM's, remained unsolved nearly twenty years later. Chrysler's product quality was the worst in Detroit. In a private report to clients, J.D. Power and Associates ranked four of Chrysler's car brands—Chrysler, Dodge, Plymouth, and Eagle—among the worst-made 1990 models sold in the United States. Chrysler also lacked geographical diversification; it was rooted in North America and needed greater access to foreign countries, where sales were growing faster. And it lagged in fuel economy; its skeletal engineering staff was struggling to cope with increasingly strict environmental regulations.

To strengthen itself, Chrysler was contemplating a merger with—who else?—Fiat. I wrote in 1990 that "the two companies are already flirting." That April, Chrysler began distributing the thirty-two-thousand-dollar Fiat-built Alfa Romeo 164 through some of its dealers, and meetings between the two companies were continuing in Highland Park, New York City, and Milan. Those meetings didn't bear fruit then, but they finally did in 2009, when Chrysler was on the ropes again.

Iacocca never troubled himself to hide his moods, and the gloom was thick when I interviewed him in March 1991. The interview took place in Chrysler's New York suite of offices in the MetLife Building, with walls lined, at Iacocca's direction, in Italian marble. The country was deep in recession, but part of the reason for Iacocca's malaise was that he had given up his treasured cigars for Lent. The combination of the cigar fast and the weak economy left him in high dudgeon.

Why was the United States having trouble with Japan? "They

start with a young work force, no health care, and no pensions. So should I go to Iowa to build a plant and screen the workers to make sure they're young and they haven't been on drugs? Do that kind of screening in Detroit, and you won't have anybody working for you."

Did he make an error shifting production sites for his small cars? "Let's say moving the Omni/Horizon cars to one plant and then to another before discontinuing them, at a cost of $100 million, was a mistake. Why argue? We made a $100 million mistake. I'm wasting $20 million every month on buyer incentives."

What happened to his heir presumptive? "Jerry Greenwald left me and got nine million dollars for a summer job."

Why was he thinking about retirement? "I can't work every day like this. It's harder than I worked ten or twenty years ago."

Pushed by his board to find a successor and move on, Iacocca couldn't bring himself to anoint Lutz (for more, see chapter 15). They didn't get along. Being considered CEO material wasn't enough for Lutz; he seemed compelled to make fun of Iacocca behind his back, and Iacocca knew it. Lutz was in the habit of speaking in French with top engineer François Castaing in front of an uncomprehending Iacocca, I reported, infuriating the CEO. A former Chrysler executive and Iacocca buddy explained their rivalry succinctly: "One hot dog can't like another hot dog."

So Iacocca went outside Chrysler to hire Robert J. Eaton, who was running GM Europe. Eaton was a curious man, and his selection would prove to be a curious choice. Yet, even with a successor in place, Iacocca remained reluctant to leave the stage. "Remember, the board didn't ask me to step aside," he told me in a remarkable but characteristic burst of candor. "I'm still virile and strong, and I want to see this company do more than just get by. It's [Eaton's] show to run, but I know the press better, the bankers better, the Washington people. I've got to use that because it's good for the company."

Easton spent nine months at Chrysler before succeeding Iacocca as chairman and CEO in 1993. Outsiders were making odds on how long it would be before Iacocca reached the conclusion that Eaton wasn't up to the job and that he, Iacocca , was irreplaceable. As one former Chrysler executive saw it: "The longer Lee lives with this guy, the longer he has to find fault with him." Another former executive added: "I can just see Lee coming to the board and saying, 'You're going to have to prevail upon me to stay because these two guys [Eaton and Lutz] are at each other's throats, and you need me to save the company.'"

By January 1, 1993, Iacocca finally did move aside. Clearly unhappy to be away from the action, though, he would actively kibitz from the sidelines for a decade—mostly unsuccessfully but always colorfully. It wasn't surprising that he was back in the news again for the umpteenth time during the Chrysler bankruptcy, when Chrysler really did link up with Fiat. Iacocca loved the spotlight, and the spotlight loved Iacocca.

CHAPTER 8

Bob Stempel and the Crisis of '92

Though Iacocca-like procrastination would have been unthinkable at buttoned-up GM, Roger Smith made his own mistakes when it came to succession. Whether consciously or not, he picked somebody as different from himself as possible. Smith ignored the leading candidate from the finance staff, another Smith named F. Alan, and set up a bakeoff between two vehicle engineers—"car guys," in Detroit parlance. It may have been the right idea, but it came at the wrong time. A savage recession was about to scorch the economy, and the man at the top of the company was unable to cope. He plunged GM into its biggest crisis since the 1920s.

Smith retired on August 1, 1990, and left the company, declining to remain on the board of directors as his predecessors had. He must have sensed that he wouldn't be welcome after what he had put GM through the previous decade. Bob Stempel replaced him as chairman and CEO. Stempel was a different sort. Decent, diligent, and well-liked, he had checked off all the boxes on his way to the top. Like Sloan, he had trained as an engineer. He had moved up through the engineering ranks, the first GM CEO ever to do that, and after stints at the head of Pontiac and Chevrolet and a

tour overseas, he ran Buick-Oldsmobile-Cadillac, the most successful of the three groups formed in the wake of the reorganization,
before being made president of the company.

Under ordinary circumstances, Stempel would have had a difficult time, given GM's competitive shortcomings. Market share had
declined precipitously under Smith, falling from 43.5 percent to 33.5
percent, and the company belatedly was cutting capacity to com-
pensate. Then, almost immediately, things got worse. One day after
Stempel took over, as he liked to remind people later, Iraq invaded
Kuwait. That set off a new oil crisis and sent the economy into a
tailspin. GM still had too many factories with the capacity to make
too many cars, and they needed to be shuttered. That was hard on
Stempel in two ways. A deliberate, perhaps plodding, decision-
maker, he hated to be rushed into making changes and preferred
to stick to his plan whatever the circumstances. And as a human
being he was loyal to a fault; he couldn't face the idea of laying off
people he'd worked with for years.

Nothing in Stempel's background had prepared him for such
a multipronged crisis. The pressure was enormous, and he didn't
handle it well. A big, beefy man, Stempel would become visibly
angry, his face turning red, when he became irked. He clearly had
to work to control himself. On several occasions, I was the target of
his pent-up rage. Once he forced me to sit and listen while he read
one of my articles aloud, correcting me on every point he disputed.
Nothing was wrong with that; writers need to be reminded of the
impact of their words. But Stempel's size—he was a former college
football player—and his position—he WAS CEO of General Motors, after all—created the unmistakable impression that he was
bullying me.

It was around this time that I first became aware of GM's perpetual tendency to bet on the come. Time after time it promised that it had finally learned how to make cars that people really wanted to buy and would have them on the market in a year or two, if critics would only be patient. One competitor called it the "mañana company."

That mañana tendency was exemplified by Stempel's number two and longtime ally, Lloyd Reuss. As other writers have observed, Reuss (pronounced "Royce") dressed like a riverboat gambler, with double-breasted vests and high, starched-collar shirts worn with collar pins, but underneath he was another GM suit who always saw good times just around the corner.

I remember a luncheon at the Chicago auto show one year when Reuss ordered the lights dimmed so that he could dazzle the audience with a seemingly endless number of new Buicks, Oldsmobiles, and Pontiacs. GM, he assured us, was preparing for its biggest new product blitz in history, and he expected a big upsurge in sales. It should have been beyond troubling that GM had been in the car business for nearly a century and still had difficulty making good cars. And whatever GM did, it was never enough because GM was so big. Even when the newest 25 percent of its product line was competitive, the remaining 75 percent had to be disposed of at fire-sale prices because the models were obsolete.

By the end of 1992, Stempel, Reuss, and a cadre of holdover executives from the Smith era were gone. They were pushed out in a historic revolt by the board of directors, led by retired Procter and Gamble CEO John Smale and board counsel Ira Milstein. It was a rare assertion of authority by the usually passive board and has never been repeated. When it recently came time for chairman and CEO Rick Wagoner to move on, after running up losses of eighty-two billion dollars, it wasn't the board that made the call, it was a Treasury Department appointee.

In a rare outbreak of prescience, I foresaw the problems Stempel would face in a profile published after he was named president in the September 28, 1987, issue of *Fortune*. Called "Bumps ahead for a Car Guy," it carried an unusually tough subhead: "Braking GM's long skid is a tough job. Critics are not sure he is up to it."

The article pointed out that despite his popularity, Stempel had amassed a long record of subpar performance. Both Pontiac and Chevrolet lost share during and after Stempel's tenure as general manager, and Buick-Oldsmobile-Cadillac, which he headed from 1984 to 1986, had suffered greatly from the problems of the reorganization. Meanwhile, Stempel had already gained a reputation for being excessively deliberate. I quoted one executive who said, "We would rehash things at such length that you'd wonder if we hadn't already made the decision long before we actually did." I noted that Stempel laboriously hand-printed messages to coworkers, was a compulsive note-taker, and seemed to assimilate vast amounts of data. He came off as the classroom grind who gets ahead not by virtue of his smarts or quick wit but because he works harder than everyone else.

Already, excess complexity was crippling the company. GM was selling cars under six brands; most companies made do with just two. GM also lagged behind its best competitors in global integration. Its big company selling Opels and Vauxhalls in Europe was treated as a separate operation. Toyota and Honda had been selling basically the same car on three continents for years, allowing them to focus their resources and spread their development costs over larger production volumes. It would be another decade before GM could do the same.

That was the beginning of an avalanche of GM stories. *Fortune* managing editor Marshall Loeb seemed to sense that a crisis was at hand and had me writing a GM story every eight weeks or so. He did talk me out of one idea: sending a letter to each member of the board of directors explaining what a terrible plight the company was in. We weren't trying to get involved in corporate governance, just develop new sources. Judging from subsequent events, our argument would have fallen on receptive ears.

As Stempel prepared to take over as CEO, we published another article in the April 9, 1990, issue with headline "The New Drive to Revive GM." I pointed out that GM was selling one-third fewer cars than it did in 1979, and that its U.S. market share had fallen from 46.3 percent to 34.7 percent. It was a sad day for America, I wrote: "No one—not even its competitors—can take any pleasure in the plight of General Motors." For his part in the story, Stempel played Stempel: obdurate, unshakable, inflexible. I quoted him as saying, "We made our decision to go with a long-term view. We just have to stay the course in North America."

That course was a one-way ticket to Palookaville, as I learned from an internal profitability analysis of GM's car lines. I can't remember ever getting my hands on any company information nearly as sensitive. Unlike the federal government, the auto industry is not full of leakers, since the disclosure of sensitive information, such as future product plans, can be damaging to the employer. The surfacing of the profitability analysis was so rare and so timely that several *Fortune* editors feared it might be a phony, planted with the hope that we would damage our credibility by publishing it. But the level of detail convinced me that the report, which I had received from a friendly securities analyst, was genuine, and by checking back through GM sources, we verified the accuracy of the information.

What the analysis showed was just how far out of line GM's product development costs had become. GM was spending far more on engineering and building its cars than it could hope to recoup by selling them. The calculations had been made for projected volumes in the 1989 model year, which had been a strong one for auto sales, and they were shocking. On a fully accounted basis, that is, when corporate overhead and development costs were included, GM expected to lose a billion dollars—a huge sum at the time.

The most unprofitable lines were low-volume specialty cars, which bore a heavy load of corporate overhead when calculated on a per-unit basis. Losses on the $52,500 Cadillac Allanté approached $8,000 a unit, and on the less expensive Buick Reatta, they were an unsustainable $17,000 a car. But even some high-volume midsize cars like the GM-10 cars were money losers. GM expected to lose $2,117 on every Chevy Lumina it made and $1,697 on every Pontiac Grand Prix.

Costs and revenue weren't GM's only problems. Its ineptitude at the basics of the car business was becoming a Detroit scandal. GM couldn't engineer and manufacture new models on any kind of schedule. For instance, after testing the new Lumina arriving at dealers side by side against the five-year-old Ford Taurus, *Consumer Reports* declared the Taurus the winner. Actually, that shouldn't have been a surprise, since the Lumina was originally designed as a 1982 model but had been delayed for seven years by budget problems and production snafus.

GM still had a structure far larger than it needed for the number of cars it was selling. In one of his earliest reports, Jim Harbour, a Detroit manufacturing consultant, reported that if GM were as efficient as Ford, never mind Toyota, it would require 60,000 fewer manufacturing workers than the 419,000 it was employing. But Stempel wasn't budging from his plan to deliberately refocus the company. "One reorganization is enough for anyone's lifetime," I quoted him as saying.

While GM remained preoccupied by its internal problems, the world around it was changing. In the fall of 1990, Loeb sent me to Japan to report on that country's largest automaker. I came back with a story that wound up leading the November 19 issue, entitled, "Why Toyota Keeps Getting Better and Better and Better." On the cover was a picture of the Lexus LS 400, introduced the year before at the remarkably inexpensive price (thanks to the cheap yen) of thirty-five thousand dollars. Inside, the story opened on a two-page spread with a picture of a fleet of Toyota cars being driven off a car carrier at a California port. If anyone in Detroit was paying attention (and I don't recall hearing from anybody at GM about it), the implied threat to American hegemony should have been chilling.

Betting on the Japanese to succeed was a theme I consistently promoted that has mostly proven correct. But I'm not always that smart. Exhibit A is a less-than-thoughtful *Fortune* piece in 1991 with the headline "How Buick Is Bouncing Back." I was anxious to write a positive GM story, and this one looked easy to pull together;

Buick was only too happy to share the good news. Its sales were up, and it was the only GM division to show an increase in market share in the 1991 model year. I attributed its bump in sales to inspired leadership by Buick's general manager and a recognition by its customers (among the oldest in the industry) of Buick's traditional American values.

In fact, Buick was benefiting because it was adding new models, like the 1992 Roadmaster, to its existing line. New models are nice, but they are like steroids: they give sales an artificial boost because they are by definition additive. Take them away, and Buick sales were right back in the doldrums. And once those new models began to age, their sales sank, too. Sales increases are best when they can be achieved organically with existing models; for new designs to have a lasting impact, they have to generate sales again and again.

My crystal ball turned even cloudier when I foresaw a similar rebound at Oldsmobile. I speculated that it "may break out of its slump" by following Buick's example: sharply defining its position in the market and then developing cars to fit it. Olds never did get its act together, and GM decided to close the division in 2000. Buick survives today with a shrunken product lineup largely because its brand has appeal in fast-growing China, where GM has staked a good part of its future.

As 1991 wore on and GM slid deeper into the red, Stempel's unchanging response was to counsel patience. He kept insisting that the company was in fundamentally good shape and what it mainly needed was an end to the recession. But he continued the gradual downsizing that Smith had begun in 1986. In October, GM announced the closure of seven assembly plants.

The UAW was not complaining about the layoffs because Stempel had bought them off. Early in his tenure, with sales plummeting and inventories of unsold cars piling up, Stempel had a fabulous opportunity to take on the UAW and roll back some of its gold-plated benefits. If it meant taking a strike, well, GM wasn't selling many cars anyway. Instead Stempel caved and promised for the first time to pay workers who weren't working as GM adjusted production to meet slumping demand. The March 1990 contract guaranteed pay to three hundred thousand laid-off workers up to 95 percent of their salary for as long as three years. The contract destroyed GM's ability to control the cost of its workforce. It had made labor a fixed cost and put GM on the hook for more than three billion dollars. Stempel characteristically called the contract a "win-win" and defied efforts to describe it otherwise.

The union always seemed to get the best of General Motors. It was smart, focused, and determined, knowing always what it wanted and where GM's pressure points were located. It was helped enormously by the structure of the industry that left GM vulnerable when only a handful of plants were shut down. A shortage of parts would ripple through the production system, forcing GM to stop building cars—and to stop generating revenue. Capitulation by the company was never far away once the union walked off the job.

The UAW never apologized for its actions, even in times of economic stress. In one of my rare interviews with a union rep—the union wasn't terribly press-friendly—a spokesperson argued that it was the union's duty to make unreasonable demands against the company because only the economic pressure they created would force GM to become more competitive against foreign automak-

111

ers. In truth, the union never believed that anything it did was unreasonable. It had convinced itself—and whoever would listen—that work in an auto plant was so deadening and dehumanizing that its members deserved anything they could get.

Besides amassing a pile of benefits that would make a sultan blush, the UAW won job guarantees that made it expensive and difficult to close plants and lay off workers. So GM was perpetually behind the curve and faced with overcapacity when it tried to downsize its operations as its market share fell. To make matters worse, GM decided that it was less expensive to make cars than to close plants, so it dumped cars into rental fleets for little or no profit rather than try to shutter a plant and pay union workers not to work. When those rental cars made their way onto the used car market in four or six months, they competed with GM's new cars for customers.

GM's condition was visibly crumbling as the recession deepened. In December 1991, Stempel announced the closing of another twenty-one plants and the cutting of seventy-four thousand jobs. Some of the plants were ones that Roger Smith had renovated and modernized as recently as the 1980s at a cost of billions of dollars. GM hadn't needed them then and certainly didn't need them now. In the final accounting, Smith's overexpansion would cost the company for more than a decade.

Loeb kept ordering up more GM coverage. A portrait of Stempel wound up on the cover of the January 13, 1992, issue under the headline, "Can GM Remodel Itself?" For *Fortune*, which prides itself on its access to corporate America, it was the rare story that didn't involve the cooperation of its subject. Stempel and other GM executives refused to see me, but there was so much news that the story almost wrote itself. I reported that even though GM was building the best cars in its history, it lagged behind its major competitors in almost every measure of efficiency and was 40 percent less productive than Ford. Accountability was all but nonexistent. A consultant noted that fewer than a hundred of GM's salaried workers out of more than one hundred thousand were dismissed annually for poor performance. And GM, despite its poor results, continued to buy off the union rather than face it down.

Looking back, the assessment of Stempel was harsh but accurate. It noted that he was the product of a highly centralized and insular culture that, in the past, always had huge resources and abundant time to bring to bear on any problem. As a competitor put it: "GM has been operating by the philosophy that, one, there is no problem that is so intractable that we cannot solve it by throwing money at it, and two, we've got all the money in the world, and if that isn't enough, we'll get some more." But the New York Yankees free-agent strategy was no longer working. Stempel, I wrote, "sometimes gets lost in details, deliberates overlong on problems, and prefers evolutionary, not revolutionary solutions. He has refused to consider changes in the six-division marketing system and has promised never to reorganize the company."

At the end of the article, I suggested ten steps GM should be taking to reform itself: reorganize; instill accountability; promote solutions, not programs; encourage candor; rationalize the product line; get tough with the union; improve efficiency; improve flexibility; cut production engineering costs; and speed new model development. Nearly twenty years later, some of those steps still needed to be taken. As the federal government's viability report on March 30, 2008, made clear, GM needed to become faster and more nimble, make do with fewer nameplates, and hold executives accountable. Like Stempel, Rick Wagoner showed himself almost pathologically unable to move any executives aside, even when they consistently underperformed.

After the January 1992 article appeared, GM answered back. It didn't like the coverage, even if it had declined to participate. Since GM was a big advertiser as well as an important company, peace talks were called for, and Loeb arranged a sit-down. In February, he, I, and two other editors flew to Detroit for a ninety-minute meeting with Stempel and six top executives. "Stempel," wrote Loeb in an Editor's Desk column at the front of the magazine, "is clearly a close *Fortune* reader, though not always an uncritical one; he admitted filling the margins of Taylor's most recent cover story with scribbled rebuttals." The meeting produced a six-page question-and-answer story in the March 9 issue of the magazine and a picture for my personal archives of me shaking hands with Stempel, both of us smiling broadly. Eight months later, four of the six executives involved in the interview, Stempel included, would be gone, swept aside by the board of directors.

What *Fortune* didn't know at the time was that GM's board of directors had already lost faith in Stempel. Outside director John Smale was about to go on a fact-finding mission at the company, interviewing managers to assess its true condition.

Chevy general manager Jim Perkins was one of the managers Smale met. During a two-hour interview, Perkins later told *Automotive News*, it became clear that Smale was suspicious of the information that Stempel and Reuss were giving the board. Smale read some quality and customer satisfaction numbers to Perkins and asked if they sounded familiar. Perkins replied they were "all much more positive than I had reported." And Smale responded that these were the numbers the corporation was handing out to the media to show how things were improving at General Motors.

When Smale reported back to the board in March, he didn't bring good news. Costs were high, product quality was low, factories were running well below capacity, GM was slow to market, and a sweeping reorganization was needed. Stempel reacted slowly, almost stubbornly, to the news. He ignored the board's direction to move aside two executives and couldn't bring himself to dismiss Reuss, as the board wanted. Instead, he demoted Reuss from president to supervision of Saturn and the electric car project. In his place, Jack Smith was moved from international operations to become the new president and took charge of North American operations, while Smale was named head of the board's executive committee. Stempel remained in place as chairman and CEO but had effectively been given a vote of no confidence.

The new setup didn't work. Stubborn as ever, Stempel didn't take the hints that rapid change was required and proceeded in his predictable, plodding manner. With the company in dire condition, the directors decided Stempel had to go, and on October 23, he became the first GM CEO since Billy Durant to be forcibly replaced. (In 2009, Wagoner would become the second.) Jack Smith moved up to CEO, while Bill Hoglund, who had been named CFO in April, was put in charge of North America. Removal of the CEO was a historic moment in corporate governance and would soon be repeated at other companies.

In the executive upheaval, two young turks popped up on my radar screen for the first time. Rick Wagoner, thirty-nine, who had been running GM Brazil, moved up to become CFO, while Lou

Hughes, forty-five, who was in charge of GM Europe, took over international operations. Their youth, fast rise, and ties to Jack Smith immediately made them the leading candidates to succeed him as CEO. But while Wagoner made steady progress without any obvious missteps, the zealous Hughes got distracted. After rebuilding operations in Europe, he allowed them to slip again because of inattention, and he was eventually moved aside.

The changing of the guard was announced at a news conference on the ground floor of the General Motors building in New York, across Fifth Avenue from the Plaza Hotel. It was a warm day, and I recall walking east on Fifty-ninth Street from the Time & Life Building and bumping into Wagoner, whom I knew slightly, and Mike Losh, who was taking over marketing for North America. Both were tall, athletic guys, and if they had any misgivings about what they were about to undertake, their relaxed manner didn't show it.

After Jack Smith became CEO, journalistic access to him was cut off for months. He was busy and didn't like talking to the media much anyway. One full year after he took over, Smith led a road show to give a progress report to securities analysts and the media. The event was held at the Rye Town Hilton in suburban Rye, New York. I don't recall what Smith and his team had to say that day, but I do remember looking at the new models GM parked outside the conference room, particularly the 1995 Chevy Lumina. Although it wasn't to be introduced for another year, it already looked bland and nondescript. For GM, as it turned out, the Lumina was a harbinger of the Smith era.

I didn't know it then, but GM had deliberately made its designs more conservative to reduce risk and appeal to the broadest possible segment of the market. This was a sensible strategy for a dominant player like GM that needed to sell a lot of cars. But GM never explained it, and it led people like me to discount the sales impact of GM cars and to complain later on about how few hit cars GM was turning out. It also put GM in a bad light compared to much-smaller Chrysler, which was emerging from its own financial crisis with exciting new vehicles like the cab-forward LH sedans and the Jeep Grand Cherokee, the first luxury mass-market SUV. With a smaller slice of the market, Chrysler was able to aim for more style-conscious buyers.

GM board member Thomas Wyman, the former CBS chairman, would occasionally give me off-the-record background on Smith's performance and GM's overall condition. In one of our last conversations before his death, he described what he called the Smith-Smale era as "disappointing." He didn't refer to the design of cars like the Lumina, but he might have.

CHAPTER 9

Jack Smith's Unfinished Revolution

S mith took over GM at a good time. The recession was ending, and business was on the upswing. The prosperity of the
1990s would keep GM solidly profitable through the decade. Smith did his part, shrinking the company, consolidating
functions, and trying to remove the air of mystery about how the
company was managed with all its committees and staffs. Total
employment, which stood at 757,000 when Smith took over, had
fallen to 388,000 by the time he left in June 2000.

The consolidation was badly needed, and Smith made it a
theme of his tenure. He took over a company that, despite the
changes of the preceding dozen years, still resembled the unwieldy
assemblage put together in the 1920s. The purchasing operation
served as a measuring gauge for GM's lack of integration. In an
operation that benefits enormously from economies of scale, GM
still had twenty-seven individual purchasing departments, each
with its own rules and specifications and each paying a different
price for the same part. Smith would eventually get them all combined into one global purchasing operation, though not without
considerable difficulty.

Yet Smith wasn't strong enough, or GM's crisis wasn't severe enough, to keep stubborn factions among product engineering, design, manufacturing, and finance from undermining one another's work. Only later, after the Pontiac Aztek fiasco, when Bob Lutz took over product development, did the fully dysfunctional nature of the system emerge: how budget overruns forced designers to use cheap plastics on interiors; how nickel-and-diming by the finance department was dooming new vehicles before they even went into production; how manufacturing executives would sabotage new treatments coming out of the design studio because they were "too difficult" to fabricate.

Looking back, I continue to marvel at how long-lived GM's problems were. I quoted an analyst in a 1992 issue who pointed out that North American operations were "laden with health care costs and unfunded pension liabilities, face a hostile United Auto Workers, produce lackluster product, and suffer internal inertia." GM suffered from the same ills. Another analyst predicted that U.S. market share, 44 percent in 1982, was headed to 30 percent. It barely slowed its decline there, and kept heading downward. You could make a lot of money shorting GM's market share.

The lessons I drew from this: "Procrastination doesn't pay; more change is better than less change; and never wait for the market to bail you out." Jack Smith might have taken those lessons to heart. Rick Wagoner, too.

At first, the down-to-earth, no-nonsense Smith seemed to be just what GM needed. Bombast and bluster were not part of his personality, and his willingness to confront reality was a sharp departure from Stempel's stubborn determination to wait for better times. UAW president Steve Yokich, no friend to industry executives, once told me that Smith was the only person at GM he respected. It was a nice compliment from an unlikely source, not that the union was going to cut the company any slack.

Smith's first goal was to "stop the bleeding," and he needed to work quickly. For the first time in seventy years GM had to worry about money. GM was expected to pile up losses of fifteen billion dollars in North America in 1992, and a yearlong cost-cutting campaign had produced almost no visible results. If GM kept losing money at this rate, *Fortune* reported in November 1992, the company might not have enough cash to operate the following spring.

The early reports on Smith were consistently encouraging—and understandable to those of us in the media. Smith favored words over deeds. He was shunning quick solutions such as selling assets. Instead, he was remaking GM by dismantling and reassembling everything: product development, engineering, purchasing, manufacturing, and distribution. Smith was pushing for common parts and common systems. As a small example, he reduced the number of turn signal stalks on GM vehicles from twenty-six to eight. On a larger scale, he wanted to shrink the number of car platforms from twelve to five. He devised simple solutions to complex problems. Because new car development was chaotic, Smith created a launch center to coordinate engineering before production started.

Smith got quicker and more lasting results working with GM's income statement and balance sheet and riding an improving economy. *Fortune* reported in March 1994 that Smith might be able to chop losses by some $5.9 billion by year's end. Rebounding sales, a richer mix of products, fewer discounts, and better management accounted for two-thirds of the projected savings. GM was also getting leaner. White-collar head count was shrinking to 71,000 from 91,000 two years earlier, while the number of hourly workers was headed toward 250,000 from 304,000 fifteen months earlier. Even hard-to-please Ford CEO Red Poling, himself no slouch at cost-cutting, was impressed. "GM has made a dramatic turnaround," he said.

Smith found the old GM system of decentralized control obsolete, but he moved too slowly, as it turned out, to reform it. And given his background in finance and manufacturing, he paid too little attention to the soft sides of the business: design, marketing, and advertising. Like Roger Smith and Stempel before him, Smith also failed to address the question why GM still had divisions like Pontiac, Buick, and Oldsmobile. There just weren't enough buyers of American cars to require that level of segmentation in the upper middle part of the market that those brands represented. Besides, trying to ensure that each brand remained distinctive during a period of ever-greater commonization of parts remained a constant headache.

Maintaining the brands was a sop to traditionalists—many employees identified more strongly with the division where they worked than with the corporation that actually signed their checks—and it was wasteful. Each division required its own design studio, along with a budget for marketing and advertising and distribution to a separate group of dealers. Descriptions of brand characteristics were constantly being revised to maintain separation, with referees needed to settle disputes about which division could use which adjectives to describe itself. Was Buick "traditional American luxury" or was Cadillac?

Pulling together first purchasing then engineering and manufacturing was time consuming; what Smith started in 1993 wasn't
completed until 2005. Since the company had to keep operating
while the consolidation was going on, one executive likened it to
overhauling an airplane engine while keeping the plane in the sky.
If any sparks flew from pushing thousands of engineers together,
though, they weren't visible from the outside. GM wasn't as lucky
with its marketing divisions. Crunching Chevy, Pontiac, Olds, Buick,
Cadillac, and GMC Truck into one North American sales and
marketing group produced fireworks that could be seen for miles.
Marketing people tended to wear their brand affiliations on their
sleeves, and many felt closer ties to Chevy or Olds than they did to
GM. Besides, each unit had an important external constituency—
its dealers, who reacted loudly and publicly to any change that
threatened to undermine their status.

Like most mergers, this one made theoretical sense: putting all
the vehicle-marketing divisions under a single staff eliminated duplication, internal competition, and brand overlap, as did replacing the six people who visited dealers with a single person representing all the brands. It sounded sensible, except the dealers didn't
like the change. The owner of a Pontiac store didn't want to be
called by the same rep who was selling cars to the Buick store
down the street. He was afraid some of his competitive secrets
might go down the street, too. "It took them a while to get used to
that," John Middlebrook, vice president of marketing and advertising, admitted to me.

Individual state franchise laws, which provide dealers with extraordinary protection in dealing with automakers, gave GM an
excuse to not eliminate any brands. When it finally did get around

to shuttering Oldsmobile in 2000, GM spent a billion dollars to buy the dealers out of their franchises. Other companies, however, seemed to accomplish the same thing without so much disruption. Ford succeeded in shrinking Mercury merely by starving it of new products, while Chrysler smoothly merged Plymouth into Chrysler and Dodge and then allowed it to die quietly. Not GM. It didn't seriously attack its dealer surplus until bankruptcy in June 2009, and then it faced a huge backlash when the politically powerful dealers complained to the congressional representatives whose campaigns they had been financing for just such an eventuality.

The Saturn division was another one of those problems that never went away. New models boosted sales in 1992 while Chevy's had declined, and Chevy dealers blamed Saturn for their loss of business. Smith had mixed feelings about Saturn. He had told me that he wanted it to stick with smaller models "for the good of General Motors" and cease developing bigger ones. As Smith well knew, that wasn't what Saturn's managers had in mind, because small cars meant small or no profits. But Smith warned that if Saturn didn't move down-market, "Saturn will start chasing not only Chevrolet but Pontiac too, and we need it to chase the imports." Not surprisingly, Saturn languished early in the Smith era.

In a crisis, companies are willing to try almost anything, and with former soap salesman John Smale as nonexecutive chairman of the board, GM was exploring different ways to develop new models, since the existing system was so clearly dysfunctional. GM executives had been designing cars for themselves, with the inevitable result. As one executive put it, "We've been building cars for old people."

Instead of looking at cars as a continuum from small to big, cheap to expensive, GM decided that it would try to design specific models for specific customer segments, based on age, income, and lifestyle requirements. This technique was called "needs segmentation analysis," and it was brought to GM by a market researcher named Vince Barabba, who had worked for Kodak and the U.S. Census Bureau. Barabba carried the mind-numbing title of executive-in-charge, General Motors Business Decision Center/Corporate Information Management, and commuted to Detroit from his home in California overlooking the Pacific Ocean, which no doubt increased his mystique.

Smale was said to be "pretty excited" about the new approach, and as a journalist, I was intrigued. I figured that once GM got the identities of its individual brands sorted out, their sheer numbers could be an advantage in commanding dealership shelf space. Each brand could be tailored to appeal to a certain group of customers. Unfortunately, Barabba's system erased any continuity of design within the brands because each model was conceived in a vacuum. It also produced cars like the Aztek that seemed to have dropped to earth from outer space. All of its myriad features had been carefully market-tested, but the whole was less than the sum of its parts.

New ideas were sprouting up all over the company. At GM's manufacturing center for North America, chief Gary Cowger was experimenting with a new technique called agile manufacturing. "Successful companies have to change from leveraging muscle power to leveraging intellectual power," said Cowger, whose perpetual tan and preference for wearing gold jewelry set him apart from other GM execs. The agile concept emphasized ultraflexible production facilities, constantly shifting alliances among suppliers, producers, and customers, and direct feedback of sales data into the factories. Like needs segmentation marketing, the concept turned out to be a fad and disappeared not long thereafter. It was replaced by a more durable concept called flexible manufacturing, which enabled companies to build a variety of vehicles on a single production line. Unfortunately, GM lagged at that, too.

Brand management, another later-to-be-discredited concept, arrived at GM about the same time. Its goal was to develop an identity for each model line so that GM could sell that line at a premium without cannibalizing other model lines. "We're confident," said CEO Smith in a speech, "that each brand can be positioned for leadership in its target segments." Pontiac became the first division to adopt Procter and Gamble's practice of assigning brand managers who would direct the development and marketing of each of Pontiac's six car lines, from Sunbird to Bonneville. Other divisions followed, but brand management would turn out to be applied more easily to soap than sedans.

One of Smith's protégés, Lou Hughes, was clearly a rising star, and I headed to Germany to find out why. Hughes was intense, there was no doubt about that. A GM lifer whose passionate approach to projects had earned him the nickname "Mad Dog," Hughes wasn't willing to wait for anything or anybody. "The first thing we have to do is sell, sell, sell," he told me insistently. "Then we have to cut our costs. We have to keep pushing urgency, urgency, urgency." As head of GM Europe, he had learned German to communicate with Opel's hourly workers, immersing himself in the language for six months and forcing colleagues to speak German in meetings with him. That frustrated subordinates at first, but Hughes became so confident that he began to use the language even in conversation with English-speaking Germans.

Unlike some others from that era, Hughes took the Japanese seriously, benchmarking them for efficiency in product development and manufacturing. Hughes had read and remembered the groundbreaking study, *The Machine That Changed the World*, with its analysis of Toyota-style lean production. "We have been warning the industry, you have to get lean," Hughes told me. "The ones who didn't believe us are really suffering now."

The downside of intensity is zealotry, and that would damage Hughes's career. At first glance, it was amusing. The previous autumn, he had led his ten top executives on a five-day Outward Bound adventure. They slept in tents, crossed a river on hand-built rafts, and, at one point, lowered themselves by harness from a narrow steel bridge into a 250-foot gorge. Groused New Yorker David Herman, who was then running Opel: "That wasn't a critical moment in my relationship with my co-workers." Hughes also retained a psychologist to train executives in group dynamics. His intensity would meet its match in his pursuit of Inaki Lopez, the GM purchasing guru turned industrial spy, and Hughes's career would run off its rails.

The rapid progress of GM under Smith was winning lots of fans, not least of whom was longtime critic Maryann Keller. In her book on the leading auto companies, she concluded that, considered against Toyota and Volkswagen, GM had the best chance to win the global auto war. Among other things, GM benefited from fewer government and societal restraints, such as a prohibition against layoffs. Keller found Smith to be "a hard-worker and a shrewd thinker," with "many of the qualities that make a strong leader."

It is better to be lucky than smart, and just when he needed it, Smith got a wind at his back: an upturn in the economy that drove car sales higher combined with a stiffening in the value of the Japanese yen that made imports more expensive. "Nobody likes an economic recovery better than the auto industry," I wrote for the April 4, 1994, issue. "Recession-weary consumers who put off buying cars and trucks are returning to the market with a rush. Dealers are watching inventories shrink and profits rise. GM, Ford, and Chrysler are adding factory shifts to meet demand."

This upturn brought something that previous ones hadn't: the explosion in popularity of a new segment—sport-utility vehicles. In response to greater fuel-economy pressures on passenger cars, automakers began to expand their offerings of SUVs, which enjoyed lower mileage standards. Built on the same chassis as pickup trucks—the popular Ford Explorer was derived from the homely Ranger pickup—SUVs produced high profits, and customers liked their flexibility and utility, as well as the big truck engines. Lacking pickups in their home market, the Japanese were slow to respond and left a big hole in the market. The strong yen didn't help them. All of a sudden, Japanese cars were more expensive than American ones. The cost difference between two functionally equivalent, V-8-powered luxury sedans—the American-made Oldsmobile Aurora and the Lexus LS 400, made in Japan—was a considerable eighteen thousand dollars.

For all of his down-to-earth qualities and emphasis on deeds, not words, Smith became captivated by the blandishments of Lopez, a Basque-born purchasing expert. Smith brought Lopez over from Europe, where he had been head of purchasing, and made him the company's worldwide purchasing czar. Lopez's mission was straightforward: find less expensive parts that would lower the cost of building General Motors automobiles.

By the time he left GM a year later, the company had racked up billions in savings. Score one for Lopez. But the way he went about it made him one of the most reviled figures in the industry. He didn't care about long-standing relationships, even when those suppliers were GM subsidiaries. He put everybody who wanted to do business with GM through endless rounds of bidding, then demanded that the survivors lower their prices even further. When they complained that they couldn't meet his impossible targets without losing money, Lopez sent teams of efficiency experts to their plants to teach them how to reduce costs in the manufacturing process.

Lopez wrapped this brutal action in some mystical mumbo-jumbo that made him sound like a shaman. He called his subordinates "warriors" and insisted they follow a "warrior" diet (fresh fruits were in, meats and coffee out). To show their allegiance to Lopez, the warriors switched their wristwatches to their right hands. Lopez was unquestionably energetic and some would say charismatic, but his system sounded like smoke and mirrors when he explained it to me. Suppliers suspected Lopez of simply shopping their price quotes around town to find lower ones—a violation of industry ethics.

When Volkswagen tried to lure Lopez away from GM in 1993, its raid quickly became public knowledge, and the two companies began bidding for his services. Smith thought that he had convinced Lopez to stay by making him head of GM's North American operations—the third biggest job in the company—and called a news conference to announce his appointment. But Lopez never showed up. Instead of accepting GM's offer, he hopped a plane to VW headquarters along with, as it turned out, a lot of information about future GM vehicles. So instead of trumpeting the news that

Lopez was staying, Smith was put in the humiliating position of having to announce that he had been jilted. Legal action followed. With Hughes in the lead, GM pursued Lopez with a criminal complaint and eventually reached a legal settlement with him and VW.

Lopez aside, I was gulping the Jack Smith Kool-Aid. Smith's lack of bombast and common sense, along with the evident improvement in GM's bottom line, had made me a believer. So I proposed a big GM story to my editors that appeared on the cover of the October 17, 1994, issue of *Fortune*. Featuring a portrait of Smith, it was headlined "GM's $11,000,000,000 Turnaround," recognizing the swing in earnings since Smith had taken over. It wouldn't be the last time I allowed my personal feelings for a CEO influence my opinions about the company. As later events would show, it is a mistake under any circumstances, but projecting the capabilities of the CEO onto an entire management is especially problematic for a company as large and complex as GM.

Smith, I wrote, knew exactly what ailed GM, and his candor was appealing. Size and success, he had said, led to "complacency, myopia, and, ultimately, decline." Money became a substitute for innovation, past victories were turned into dogma, and maintenance of the status quo became the measure of success. A giant headquarters bureaucracy, under the paw of the accountants, attempted to coordinate everything but instead wound up stifling it. "'We lost touch with the customer' would probably be the kindest way to say it," said Smith.

When a company is performing well, there is an understandable impulse to attribute the success to the CEO and to examine

his actions in light of that. For instance, I praised Smith for allowing the chief designer to report to the head of engineering instead
of to the vice chairman, to whom he had previously been accountable. I concluded that now engineering and design would work
more closely together in the creation of new models. No question,
the vice chairman reporting relationship was an oddity, probably
the result of some special arrangement in past years. But putting
design under engineering meant that ease of assembly and manufacture would take precedence over creativity and style. Nearly a
decade later, product development chief Bob Lutz would have to
rescue design from dominance by engineering and allow it to report directly to him.

Nothing Smith said deterred me from my deification. I even
compared him to GM's legendary CEO Alfred Sloan, another
classic blunder. Sloan had the good sense to arrange for his own
legacy by publishing the business classic *My Years with General
Motors*. Ever since it appeared in 1963, it has been used by journalists as a guidebook for subsequent CEOs, with the result that
Sloan gets reimagined and redefined with each succeeding generation. Like Bible verses, bits of Sloan wisdom can be applied to
almost any situation.

Sadly, a lot of things that Smith promised would happen at GM
never did. For one thing, he figured that the company would get
its operations in order by 2000. That proved optimistic. As late as
2008, GM still ranked near the bottom in *Consumer Reports'* quality analysis, and GM is still trying to figure out how to get close to
its customers. For another, Smith figured that after earning a 2.7

percent return on sales in the second quarter of 1994, GM could reasonably expect to aim at a 5 percent target. That was a nice idea, but it proved unreachable. GM never got close.

Cracks in Smith's heroic facade began to appear almost immediately after *Fortune*'s October 1994 story appeared. After a period of acute embarrassment, I was required to do some aggressive backing and filling. I would like to report that I learned something from the episode and never repeated the same mistake, but that wouldn't be accurate.

CHAPTER 10

Bob Eaton's Big Score

Despite superficial similarities, Chrysler's Bob Eaton was no Jack Smith. The two men both came out of GM's international operation, where Eaton worked for Smith. Physically, they were similar, too, both on the pudgy side, though Eaton was a few inches shorter—I would guess around five feet, eight inches tall. But unlike Smith, who was revered by his coworkers and respected by journalists, Eaton had a peculiar personality that put some people off. He seemed to derive little pleasure or satisfaction from his job. His usual expression was one of vague stomach upset. I am normally polite and respectful toward news subjects in general, and CEOs in particular, and the only time I can recall being overtaken by a fit of giggling was during an Eaton news conference. Eaton saw me doing so and called me on it. I was embarrassed and apologized to him later, but it left me wondering about the existence of thin skin on this presumably powerful executive.

Eaton's colleagues found him odd, too. As journalists Bill Vlasic and Bradley Stertz reported in *Taken for a Ride* (2000), Eaton was perceived as standoffish and cold. He had come to Chrysler by himself, without even an assistant, and he remained a loner, bereft of confidants. He cut off conversations as if in a hurry to get them over. Juxtaposed against this seeming introversion was a tendency to cry in public during moments of great emotion.

For all of his impulsive actions, Iacocca had left behind the pillars of a surprisingly robust company. Most said it was because he had delegated operations of the company to the product-focused Lutz during his final months, that Iacocca "hadn't gotten in the way" of what Lutz was doing. Whatever the reason, Chrysler had caught the sweet spot of the light truck boom. Its upscaled Jeep Grand Cherokee was a huge hit, and the company was making outsize profits on its Chrysler, Dodge, and Plymouth minivans and Dodge trucks. Chrysler's new cab-forward full-size sedans, code-named LH, were doing well, too.

I took a look at Eaton's Chrysler for *Fortune*'s first issue of 1994 and came away impressed. At that moment, Chrysler was the world's most successful automaker. Two years after flirting with insolvency, it would record 1993 operating profits of about two billion dollars—more from the auto business than GM and Ford combined—or, for that matter, all nine Japanese automakers. One analyst figured that Chrysler made an average gross profit of $8,140 on each of the more than two hundred thousand Grand Cherokees it sold in 1993 and $5,735 on each of a comparable number of LH sedans. Its market share was growing, too, up to 14.8 percent from 12.0 percent in 1991.

A CEO almost always looks good when his company is doing well, and Eaton was no exception. His imperfections would surface later, but for now he was doing fine. He ran the company in an unshowy, results-oriented way, and Lutz was saying nice things about him. "Bob Eaton is the least princely CEO I have ever seen in my life," Lutz said. "He is a demanding boss, but he is not imperial." Later, Eaton and Lutz would be barely speaking to each other, but their public facade of cooperation remained intact.

I got Eaton talking about some of the newsy topics of the day, and his comments on alliances were especially revealing. Four years later, he would push Chrysler into one of the most misbegotten mergers of all time, but for now, he was opposed to projects involving two manufacturers. Said Eaton: "I believe alliances are very difficult over time. . . . You can do individual products or buy and sell with each other and be successful. But separate stock ownership in a venture—I don't think that works."

At times, Eaton seemed to be living in his own alternative universe, one that revolved around Bob Eaton. Nowhere was his tone deafness more apparent than in his dealings with maverick investor Kirk Kerkorian. Kerkorian had bought 10 percent of Chrysler's stock as a so-called passive investor, but in the spring of 1995, he decided he wanted to buy a controlling interest and launched an unsolicited tender offer. Kerkorian and Eaton had been talking regularly on the phone, but each one didn't seem to hear what the other was saying. When the buyout offer came, it caught Eaton and Chrysler off-guard. One Kerkorian insider astonishingly attributed it to a "misunderstanding" between the two men. It was hardly surprising. Kerkorian had been doing deals all his life and is said to have regarded Eaton, a University of Kansas–educated engineer, as "a bit of a farm boy" who wasn't sophisticated about financial issues or shareholder relations.

Spicing things up even further was the news that Kerkorian had enlisted Iacocca in his effort. The two men were acquaintances, and Iacocca, obviously unhappy on the sidelines, was always interested in making a buck. On the morning the news broke that the two men wanted to take over Chrysler, Eaton was scheduled to speak at the annual breakfast for journalists and public relations people at the opening of the New York auto show. Instead, he hopped a plane back to Detroit and left his spokesman Bud Liebler to deliver a short statement to several hundred reporters and deal with dozens of questions he couldn't answer. As a member of the audience, I was swept up in the chaos along with everyone else.

The next day, Eaton showed up at a ceremony at a Chrysler plant in Detroit. I was there along with hordes of other journalists, and Eaton did something very bizarre. When the ceremony ended, Eaton could have decided to stand his ground and use the platform he had been granted to make a corporate statement about the importance of Chrysler remaining in local hands and its intention to fight the takeover—an anti-Kerkorian statement. This would have been a good negotiating tactic, if nothing else. Instead, Eaton ran. He literally sprinted down the plant floor, out the door, and into his waiting car while TV cameras recorded the whole embarrassing event. Chrysler's public relations people were nonplussed.

When Kerkorian's takeover attempt foundered because of lack of financing (though not before causing long-term damage to Iacocca's reputation), Chrysler continued to ride the wave of buoyant industry sales and its own hot products. In the January 9, 1996, issue, I reported that Eaton and other company executives were saying that Chrysler had blown past Ford and GM and was set to become the country's "premier producer of cars and trucks."

But something about Chrysler was setting off warning bells, and I cautioned restraint. It was difficult to imagine any automaker, no matter how good, outperforming the rest of the industry year after year, I wrote. Markets shift, complacency and caution set in, and someone else comes along who works harder and smarter. GM was a powerhouse in the 1960s, and Ford in the 1980s, and both eventually stumbled. My comments are just as true today. Some companies, notably Toyota, Honda, and BMW, manage to perform consistently well for years, but the others exist in a boom-and-bust world that comes from changing trends, model cycles, and hit products.

Chrysler, of course, would have none of it and defiantly declared that it was special and this time was different. It was the same argument Ford would use some twelve years later when it refused federal aid. "We are so radically different that it pains me to see the fourth estate lump us together with our success-challenged competition from across town," Lutz told a group of journalists. But Eaton, Lutz and the rest of Chrysler had yet to convince Wall Street that GM and Ford were doomed to eat Chrysler's dust. Wrote one analyst, exaggerating only slightly: "When a company shows the degree of self-confidence and self-assuredness that Chrysler is, it is usually the beginning of the end."

In fact, it was the beginning of the end for Chrysler, although not for the reasons that anyone could have predicted. Daimler-Benz's Jürgen Schrempp would come calling two years later, setting in motion a decade-long marriage made in hell that, in the end, would help push Chrysler into bankruptcy in 2009.

It turned out that the brush with Kerkorian had so unsettled Eaton that he desperately wanted to erect a defense to fend off the next unwanted suitor. Daimler filled the bill. For his part, Schrempp wanted to diversify Mercedes beyond luxury cars and commercial vehicles, and after being rebuffed by Ford, he came to Chrysler in January 1998 to talk about a "merger of equals." After a meeting lasting only minutes in which Schrempp pitched the idea to Eaton, it became a done deal a few months later. Mercedes and Chrysler were joined in a new company, DaimlerChrysler.

Schrempp was one of those outsize creatures who seemed made for a big-metal business like autos. He had Iacocca's ego and ambition and none of his insecurity. An imposing man with enormous energy and an irresistible personality, he bulldozed everyone in his path. Life was an adventure for Schrempp, and he was determined to squeeze every minute of enjoyment out of it that he could. If that included carrying on a blatantly public affair with his attractive and attentive personal assistant and divorcing his wife, that was of little concern to Schrempp. He believed that rules were made for ordinary people; he himself could do anything.

On paper, the Daimler-Chrysler deal looked great to most people, including me. The two companies fit together like yin and yang. Chrysler made moderately priced passenger cars and light trucks; Daimler made Mercedes luxury cars and heavy trucks. Chrysler was strong in North America and weak in western Europe, Daimler just the reverse. Chrysler was deft at design and product development; Daimler held the upper hand in engineering and technology. Best of all, it was a marriage of opportunity, not desperation. These were not two sick companies combining to create one larger sick company. Chrysler was riding high in the U.S. car and truck boom; Daimler had restructured and was expanding at a breakneck pace.

Searching for potential flaws in this marriage-made-in-heaven scenario, the obvious worry was over the clashing of cultures—the methodical Germans, protective of the Mercedes brand, versus the freewheeling, opportunistic Americans. In the end, it doomed the merger, but when I raised the question with Schrempp and Eaton when they sat down in New York for a joint interview in May 1998, both men swatted it down.

Said Schrempp: "You know, I'm a bit amazed about the role the culture issue has played. You could not get a deal together in four months if you didn't think the same, and the chemistry was right on both sides. Added Eaton: "We had exactly the same thing. Chrysler has really done a lot of adapting of its culture, and it has been very inclusive. I'm not underplaying the culture situation, but I do believe that currently it is being overplayed."

The issue of who would be the dominant partner was quickly settled. The new company was incorporated in Germany and run mostly by former Daimler executives. Schrempp shared the title of cochairman with Eaton, who immediately made himself a lame duck by announcing that he would retire in three years. Chrysler executives had already begun to gripe about their Daimler colleagues' habit of concluding negotiations by saying, "No, this is how we will do it—end of discussion."

One warning sign of the difficulties to come should have been the creation of the "brand bible." Worried about protecting the Mercedes name, Daimler insisted on compiling detailed rules for each car brand that determined not only the retail distribution market by market but also research and development, purchasing, production, and marketing. The rules set guidelines, for example, about when a brand would get new technology. Leading the effort was Mercedes's up-and-coming marketing chief Dieter Zetsche, who usually wore a broad smile to go with his extravagantly bushy moustache and who took the new regulations very seriously. "The rules have been agreed upon between the sales organizations and approved by the board, and are now law," he said. But in doing so, he created a bone of contention with Chrysler's freewheeling managers.

It didn't help that Eaton, in an unintentional masterstroke, had sold Chrysler at the peak. The economy was weakening, and Chrysler's super-hit cars and SUVs were aging. Sales fell off quickly, and Schrempp had a problem on his hands. With Eaton gone by late 2000, he fired Chrysler CEO Jim Holden and replaced him with Zetsche. Then he confessed that all the happy talk about a true partnership was just that—happy talk. "It was in spirit a merger of equals," Schrempp was saying now. "However, we are living in a changing world." Schrempp conceded that the atmosphere at Chrysler with a German in charge "was not cozy." But he continued to argue that the merger would pay off, brandishing charts that showed big savings from joint projects like sharing power trains across Mercedes and Chrysler vehicles. Though some management board members were reportedly discussing the idea of selling off part of Chrysler, Schrempp adamantly rejected the idea. "It would be the nth degree of stupidity," he said. "Why should I give up on a fantastic strategy because I have a problem?"

Schrempp already had moved on to his next thing—trying to arrange linkups with Nissan and Hyundai to form a global company—and left the messy operational details of making the merger work to subordinates. Still, Zetsche seemed to be an inspired choice. An engineer with a strong marketing background, he combined an intense intelligence with an instinctive flair for personal relations and a self-deprecating sense of humor. I had encountered him several times over the previous decade as he moved through a series of jobs at Mercedes and never failed to be charmed by his candor, wit, and the literal twinkle in his eye. Chrysler and the rest of Detroit quickly warmed to him as well; Zetsche's willingness to plunge into civic affairs made him the most popular CEO in town.

I thought Zetsche had a surefire formula for getting Chrysler back on track. He said all the right things. Chrysler quality was still—still!—below industry standard, and he declared that he was determined to fix it. Zetsche set a target for the whole company to reach Toyota-level quality with 25 percent fewer defects by 2006. Unfortunately, Toyota proved to be a moving target, and Chrysler continues to have the worst quality of any major automaker selling in the United States.

Zetsche also promised to do more with less. Specifically, he wanted to cut the company's five-year, forty-three-billion-dollar capital-spending plan to thirty billion, yet still add five new vehicles to Chrysler's lineup. That would be the automotive equivalent of getting dozens of clowns to climb out of a tiny circus car. New models drive dealer traffic and sales, but each one requires an investment of up to a billion dollars and a lead time of three to four years. Squeezing so much more out of a capital budget suggested that Zetsche had found a breakthrough.

Zetsche got his cars out, but the results were disappointing. He launched one bona fide hit, the Chrysler 300, which was based on running gear from the Mercedes E-class. The "C" version powered by Chrysler's popular V-8 "Hemi" engine became a cult favorite. Other models developed alongside the 300, though, were not as popular, and Zetsche, trying to extend Chrysler's brands on the cheap, created a number of duds. Half a dozen of them were derivatives of existing models that had eye-catching but cheesy styling and bargain-basement interiors.

A special place in the Chrysler Hall of Shame should be reserved for the executive, whether Zetsche or somebody else (nobody's stepped up to take credit for it), who green-lighted the Sebring sedan for introduction in 2006. Designed to compete against the Toyota Camry and the Honda Accord in the midsize segment, the Sebring flopped by trying to combine the virtues of a higher "command" seating position with traditional four-door styling. The awkward design satisfied no one, and Chrysler for awhile was contemplating stopping production on the Sebring in 2009 after just three years on the market—a remarkable admission of failure.

Zetsche produced another burst of positive earnings but couldn't consistently repeat the results. Still, his performance was timely enough, so that when Schrempp retired unexpectedly in 2005 as chairman of DaimlerChrysler, Zetsche was named to replace him. With Zetsche called back in Germany, emotional ties between Daimler and Chrysler were frayed. Shortly thereafter, the UAW failed to grant Chrysler the same contract concessions it had extended to GM and Ford, arguing (correctly) that Daimler had deeper corporate pockets. Daimler took that as a signal that it would never be able to make Chrysler cost-competitive and put the company up for sale in 2007.

The winning bidder was Cerberus Capital Management, a New York–based private equity investor. Daimler was so eager to be rid of Chrysler's obligations to retired autoworkers that it effectively gave 80 percent of the company away for nothing. Its thirty-seven-billion-dollar investment was valued at zero. Cerberus loaded

Chrysler up with debt to finance its operations and installed a seasoned manager, former GE and Home Depot executive Bob Nardelli, as CEO. Very quickly it became apparent that its timing was disastrous; Cerberus had bought Chrysler just as the United States was slipping into a deep and prolonged recession. Nardelli couldn't cut costs fast enough as sales fell 40 percent and more a month. After intervention by the federal government, Chrysler declared bankruptcy on April 30, 2009.

Most auto people weren't wild about Nardelli. His tenure at Home Depot had ended unhappily, and he wasn't a car guy. The reports coming out of Chrysler weren't encouraging, either. Nardelli liked to remind people who the boss was, and one executive described him as a "heads I win, tails you lose" decision-maker. By the end of his tenure, there were so many empty desks and vacant offices at Chrysler that basic operations required for the future of the company were in jeopardy.

I saw Nardelli several times at Chrysler, and although his interactions with the media seemed coached and unnaturally formal, I never found him unpleasant. Like many Detroit outsiders, he was astounded by many practices that auto people considered normal and even necessary, such as Chrysler's participation in more than sixty auto shows. Given more time and more resources, as well as a willingness to listen to his product planners and engineers, Nardelli might have turned Chrysler around—or at least stopped its slide. Instead, in 2009 a bankruptcy court judge effectively took over as Chrysler's CEO and helped arrange its sale to Fiat.

Fiat CEO Sergio Marchionne moved in immediately, reorganizing top management and planning future products. He exuded confidence, but his best hope for success rested with the recovery of industry sales since Fiat would need two years before it could make meaningful improvements in Chrysler's lineup. Chrysler had little in the way of new models to promote and would have to struggle to meet stricter government fuel economy regulations. Marchionne insisted that he could turn around the company and double its sales, but after eight decades in the car business, Chrysler's existence was more fragile than ever.

CHAPTER 11

GM on Cruise Control

The *Sports Illustrated* cover jinx hit *Fortune* in 1994—and Jack Smith. Within days after our glowing story appeared in the October 17 issue, GM was rocked by two pieces of bad news. First, the company surprised Wall Street on October 20 by revealing that it earned just $552 million on sales of $34.5 billion in the third quarter—mainly because its core North American auto operations lost $328 million. In two disastrous days, GM stock skidded 12 percent, to a new twelve-month low near forty-one dollars a share. All of a sudden, Jack Smith didn't look so smart.

Worse, GM had found a different way to foul up: it was botching the launch of new models, a fundamental part of the business and one that Toyota and Honda executed flawlessly. Production of the Chevrolet Cavalier and its sister Pontiac Sunfire had begun at GM's plant in Lordstown, Ohio, in August 1994 but wouldn't reach full capacity of eighty-four cars an hour until midsummer 1995, months behind schedule. There were two major stumbling blocks: a new flexible system for stamping and assembling sheet-metal bodies that produced ill-fitting panels, and a Japanese lean-production blueprint that flopped when translated into GM-ese.

The Lordstown fiasco would cost GM more than two billion

dollars in lost sales and a point of market share. Publicly at least, GM's top brass had expressed no concerns before the news hit, which raised questions about whether a company as large as GM, with 346,200 employees in the United States and Canada, had the systems in place—or the necessary culture—to know what was going on everywhere in its empire and to keep Smith informed. Smith dismissed the idea that he was out of the loop, but Lordstown had clearly become a sensitive topic. "Are we disappointed we don't have the cars?" he asked. "You bet we are. But we're not going to get rid of people down there. Our guys did a pretty good job. The point is, we've got to do better than that."

Fortune's editors weren't pleased that a company we had written so admiringly about wasn't able to execute such a basic operation as starting up production of a new model, and I wasn't either. My article was the object of critical remarks in auto industry trade publications and elsewhere. Said the *Wall Street Journal:* "So much for the GM turnaround story." There wasn't much I could do about it. Anytime you write an article, you are subject to second-guessing. Also, the production foul-up had a deus ex machina feeling about it. There was no way I could have predicted it; GM had done nothing like that in its recent history, and the possibility hadn't turned up in my reporting. Still, an incident like that causes you to question your judgment or make you a little gun-shy. It also ensures you are much more careful the next time.

Fortune's new managing editor, John Huey, thought we ought to explain ourselves in print. I wasn't wild about his suggestion, but I did see the wisdom of it. A veteran of the *Wall Street Journal*, Huey combined a marvelous ability to cultivate important sources with a knack for finding a compelling story line in almost any news event. He is the best journalist I ever worked for and would go on to become editor in chief of Time Inc., overseeing more than one hundred magazines.

My mea culpa, which appeared in our May 29, 1995, issue, didn't go far. I conceded a few points but defended myself on many others. Rereading it fourteen years later, I didn't find it very convincing.

I reported that Smith and his team appeared relaxed and confident (another mistake: even when they are on the defensive or under stress, executives almost always look relaxed and confident; that's part of their job) and declared that GM's turnaround was proceeding on schedule. As for those nasty production problems, I wrote, "Factories aren't running smoothly because they are being massively overhauled for greater productivity and flexibility. New models are slow to emerge because product development is being revamped and quality standards are higher." That may have been true, but it was no excuse. GM was repeating a favorite rationalization: the cars were late coming out of the plant because it wanted to get the quality exactly right.

I argued that the glass wasn't half empty at GM, it was half full. As evidence, I noted GM had made $1.1 billion in North America during 1995's first three months. The same old problems kept turning up, however. Quality, efficiency, and productivity, though improving, were still not up to the best in the world. An unfunded pension liability loomed, and health care costs were a growing financial burden. GM was negligent in weeding out underperformers among its employees. And the product lineup still had holes. The midsize Olds Cutlass Ciera and Buick Century were based on engineering that was fifteen years old—a major shortcoming when the Japanese competition was bringing out all-new cars every eight years.

My conclusion was somewhat counterintuitive: GM had great potential because there was a lot left to fix. "Perhaps the biggest reason for a brighter outlook at GM is that there is so much room for improvement." A security analyst I quoted had a much better read on it. As he put it, "GM is going from pathetic to mediocre."

One place where GM had a big opportunity to do better was in restoring the health of its brands and how they were marketed. Pontiac had adopted Procter and Gamble's practice of assigning brand managers for each of its six car lines, and they began to dig more deeply into the product development process. They defined brand characteristics and styling cues—lower-body plastic cladding and split grilles in Pontiac's case—and started to oversee advertising for the life span of a given model. It sounded sensible, like assigning a single doctor instead of a team of specialists to look after the health of the patient. But it also revealed a mechanistic approach to designing and selling cars that dated back to Roger Smith—adding overhead and complexity rather than just making more distinctive vehicles. And by demanding the same styling cues across an entire product line, the brand managers tended to make cars into caricatures: all Pontiacs came with lower cladding, all Saturns had plastic bodies. Purists, including some inside GM, were appalled. Smale, they were convinced, had it wrong. The individual car models weren't the brands, the divisions were. Nobody came into a showroom wanting to see the new Grand Am—they wanted to see a Pontiac!

As brand managers multiplied, a new challenge emerged:

keeping them from getting in each other's way. After all, they all couldn't go after the same desirable demographic slice for their brands—the young couple in their thirties with an "active lifestyle" who were always rushing off to the mountains or the beach, trailing mountain bikes and surfboards in their wake. Since communication, coordination, and cooperation all seemed to be out of the question, GM devised yet another bureaucratic solution. It set up a new department, the Marketing Assessment Center, to help the brand managers keep track of the public images of all the models that GM sold. The center's job was to make sure that different divisions didn't advertise on the same television shows or look for promotion at the same sports events.

Clearly, a GM lifer would be out of his or her depth in this brave new world of brand marketing. So Smale went outside the company in late 1994 to hire Ron Zarella, a confident, round-faced man who had been selling eyeglasses and contact lenses at Bausch and Lomb. Zarella ran marketing and was, in turn, tasked with recruiting brand managers. Some of the brighter lights from inside GM applied for these brand jobs, but Zarella made sure each division got at least one manager from outside the company, places such as General Foods, Nabisco, and Gerber.

The brand managers did some weird stuff. The brand manager for the new Cadillac Catera reportedly rejiggered Cadillac's traditional "wreath and crest" emblem by taking one of the six birds facing left, turning it around, coloring it red, and making it into a cartoon mascot. His aim? To attract baby boomers by projecting an irreverent image intended to show that the Catera was far removed from the stodgy Cadillac of old. It didn't work. Reengineered from a German Opel, the overweight, underpowered Catera flopped along with its irreverent brand management tagline, "The Caddy that zigs."

The ambitious Zarella did have the refreshing habit of speaking his mind on occasion, and as an outsider he enjoyed taking shots at entrenched industry practices. He aroused the ire of dealers by speculating publicly about the future of auto sales on the Internet and expressed worries about big, public dealer groups such as AutoNation controlling GM's distribution. I liked him because he ruffled feathers. At one GM event, he publicly mused over dinner whether the popular but old-fashioned Cadillac DeVille would fit with New Age Caddies like the edgy CTS. Other executives played down Zarella's comments, but he was prescient, if a bit premature. Rechristened the DTS, the DeVille was out of place in Cadillac's new lineup and would be killed at the end of the 2009 model year.

Over time, however, Zarella became associated with a number of flops. Jack Smith scored a triumph when he ordered the development of shorter versions of the Chevy Suburban to capitalize on the SUV boom, and gave birth to the Chevy Tahoe and GMC Yukon. They turned out to be huge moneymakers. But when GM tried a similar stunt during the Zarella era by stretching the GMC Envoy and adding a third row of seats, the result was a strangely elongated vehicle that filled a need nobody had. Further muddying the waters was the creation of a niche model, the XUV, with a sliding rear roof in place of the tailgate. It was perfect for hauling around tall plants but not much else. Sales were projected at thirty thousand per year but were much slower, and it was quietly discontinued within a few years.

Zarella also had the misfortune to be associated with the Pontiac Aztek, one of the least attractive vehicles GM—or anyone else—has ever built. I was in the audience at GM's Tech Center in Warren, Michigan, on the day in October 1999 when GM revealed the production version of the Aztek to the press. The company was positioning the minivan/SUV as a "lifestyle support vehicle" for those elusive active thirty-year-olds that was the "most versatile vehicle on the planet." Our curiosity piqued, we watched as the drapes were pulled off the car—and then the room went strangely silent. The Aztek bristled with creases, roof racks, and plastic cladding—and that was the good news. A toxic mix of overreach by market research, compromises by manufacturing, and penny-pinching by finance had produced a vehicle that appealed to practically no one. Within weeks, the Aztek would be judged one of the ugliest cars of all time. The fundamental mission of any auto company is creating cars that people want to buy, and GM had failed with the Aztek.

At first, Zarella defended the homely Aztek. When sales ran at 2,500 a month instead of the 4,000 a month GM planned for, he said the van was priced too high and moved production to Mexico to take advantage of lower costs. Then he said that adding larger wheels and tires along with monochrome body cladding would make it look more appealing. But nothing worked. GM had forecast sales of up to 75,000 Azteks per year and needed to produce 30,000 annually to break even. Just 27,322 were sold in 2001, with more than 50 percent reportedly going to rental company fleets or General Motors employees. To the relief of everyone, the vehicle was discontinued in the 2005 model year.

GM's new marketing push wasn't helped by its ability to find new ways to irritate its dealers. GM installed a computerized system that required them to order cars up to ninety days in advance and made changes difficult. When the system collapsed one month, the dealers couldn't order anything at all, and sales tumbled. The computers eventually got fixed, but there were other areas of conflict. GM was trying to take over local dealer advertising cooperatives to coordinate its ad effort and get volume discounts. But in so doing, it lost contact with individual market variations, and the efficiency of the advertising declined. Then GM decided to go into competition with its own dealers by announcing plans to buy as many as seven hundred outlets and run them itself. After a huge outcry, it backed off. "In hindsight, those were both mistakes," an executive later admitted.

When the heat from the dealers got too intense, CEO Smith was called in to put down a rebellion. At a meeting in January 2000, he made a public apology. It was the beginning of the end for Zarella, who would leave GM in November 2001 to go back to Bausch and Lomb. "Rick [Wagoner, then head of North American operations] stood behind Ron," I quoted Smith saying afterward. "But that's not to say the dealers weren't happy when [Ron] left. They didn't like Ron. The car business is so unique. You can come in as an outsider and look at some things and say, 'That's really a dumb way to run.' But the unfortunate thing is, that is the way it runs. There are some things you just have to live with."

Ever loyal, Wagoner took part of the blame. "Was some of that [Zarella's] fault?" he said later. "Sure. But did we give him the right mentoring, did somebody step in and say, 'Be careful about going the wrong way with the dealers?' Maybe guys like me or Jack didn't do enough."

Zarella was history, and by 2002, so was brand management. "The brand is the division," declared John Middlebrook, a GM veteran who would take over marketing activities. "At the end of the day, we've got to drive traffic to the store, and the store is where the divisional name is displayed."

Jack Smith was beginning to seem out of touch as his term as CEO wore on, or at least not tackling them with his old intensity. He seemed tired out by frequent trips to Asia to get GM's China operations moving. Signs of his inattention were growing. There was a vicious and vengeful strike by the United Auto Workers in 1998, which all but stopped GM's North American operations for two months. It grew out of an ill-considered effort to win a bargaining dispute with a Flint stamping plant. After talks broke down, GM reversed a plan to install new transfer presses at the plant and began pulling out critical dies, prompting the UAW to strike. Within two weeks, GM assembly plants across the company that were supplied from Flint were shut down, too. The strike cost $2.8 billion in second-quarter profits and reinforced GM's bumbling image. As it typically did in confrontations with the union, GM came away empty-handed in the settlement. GM installed the transfer presses with the dies, and the union went back to work.

In *Fortune*'s August 3, 1998, issue, I wrote that the Smith team had lost its momentum and declared that it was time for another revolution. GM continued to underperform competitors. Its ability to execute even such basic functions as launching new vehicles on time remained in question. Europe, the shining light of GM's global empire earlier in this decade, was struggling. The question I asked: Were Smith, an old-looking sixty, and his handpicked executive team up to the job?

There was plenty of evidence to support my argument. GM had responded sluggishly to changes in the market, such as the boom in sport-utility vehicles. Four of its seven car and truck divisions—Saturn, Pontiac, Buick, and Cadillac—sold no SUVs at all. There was no accountability. Employees guilty of mistakes—and there were plenty—were never identified, and ritual hangings were as rare as a snowless winter in Michigan. Interdivisional squabbling was consuming time and resources. The ongoing battle between GMC and Cadillac over which division would sell the more upscale sport-utility vehicle was just one example. And Smith seemed indecisive. While Saturn waited for new product, sales of its three existing models dried up because they weren't updated frequently enough.

Unable to gain access to Smith or any other GM executives for this story, I was reduced to peering in from the outside. But the absence of any signs of intensity seemed telling. GM needed a jolt from a dramatic action, like a reorganization, a new statement of purpose, or a public execution or two. But getting out front was just not Smith's style. I quoted John Kotter, professor of leadership at Harvard Business School, as saying: "How often have you heard of Jack Smith standing up in front of a meeting and telling 500 people that there is a war going on in the global auto industry, and that they have been losing this war for a decade and it's not acceptable? He ought to be doing that once a week. And he ought to be begging everybody around him to do the same thing."

In another familiar trope, GM continued to be so blinded by its past success that it couldn't see a different future. Instead of the 35 percent market share GM expected, its portion of U.S. sales continued to slip under Smith's tenure, shrinking to 31.1 percent in 1997. But GM still maintained the infrastructure to support a larger company. "GM's plight practically screams for a leader who can move quickly and decisively," I wrote. Harvard's Kotter could barely contain himself. "GM is such a sad case. You've got denial, complacency, depression—everything except urgency." University of Michigan professor Noel Tichy, an adviser to GE's Jack Welch, believed that radical action was required. Said he: "I have yet to see a CEO who says, 'I went too fast, I should have moved more slowly.' Resistance to change is deeply embedded in GM. You can make a decision at the end of the train track and people will pull switches in front of you to keep you from getting there."

Even compared to its crosstown rivals, GM was performing sluggishly. GM made a record $6.7 billion in earnings in 1997, but that produced a net margin of just 3.9 percent, disturbingly low in what was a strong year for auto sales. The company failed to match Ford's $6.9 billion in profits even though Ford reported $25 billion less in revenues. GM's stock, not surprisingly, had performed dismally. Since Smith took over on November 2, 1992, the company's return to shareholders had been 167.5 percent, versus 404.5 percent for Chrysler and a stunning 497.6 percent for Ford. At GM's core North American operations, the numbers were even worse. GM's revenue per vehicle lagged behind Ford's and Chrysler's, in part because GM products tended to generate less customer appeal. In profit per vehicle, GM made much less than Chrysler because of its high costs and was falling further behind Ford. Although worker productivity at GM plants showed signs of improvement, it still fell short of Ford's and was not even in the same league as Toyota's and Honda's.

As I got deeper into my reporting, I could see that GM was

blaming history for its problems. Founder Billy Durant, who had assembled GM from individual vehicle and component manufacturers, got the brunt of it. As one executive griped: "The die was cast 70 years ago when everything was bought, rather than built from within." Wagoner would return to that theme a decade later. His explanation for GM's troubles was that companies, like ships, tend to attract barnacles the longer they are in the water and that GM was handicapped by the obligations it had accumulated in its hundred-year history.

By the time Smith announced his intention to give up the CEO's job on June 1, 2000, the identity of his successor was long known. The steady, self-effacing Wagoner, in many ways a man in Smith's mold, had been named president back in 1998. His chief rival, Hughes, had been done in by his obsessive prosecution of Inaki Lopez combined with his inattention to international operations at a time when a financial crisis was squeezing results. Hughes was moved into a vague global strategy position when Wagoner was elevated to president and then left the company in April 2000.

Fortune detected disappointment when the news about Wagoner was disclosed. We reported that he was a team player when what GM really needed was a Vince Lombardi. An outsider, of course, was never considered for the job and the received wisdom was that it was an impossible one for anyone not steeped in GM's ways. *Fortune* quoted Wagoner as saying, "An outsider could never come in here and figure it all out." That was six years before Alan Mulally left the aerospace industry to straighten out Ford.

Wagoner was surprisingly candid in assessing the Smith years when I interviewed him for an article in the April 5, 2004, issue. He blamed some of GM's shortcomings since 1992 on driver error, but others he attributed to unavoidable potholes along the way. "We made huge progress in '92, '93, '94, but then we started to pay the price because we had, out of necessity, underspent [on new products] during that tight period and didn't do that well on the revenue side. Then, in the last three or four years, we've run the business very well, but the pricing has been tough." Wagoner's conclusion: "This is not a one-step game. This is a multiple[-year] thing, and it's hard, and you learn as you go along."

GM still needed to move faster and smarter. One lesson it hadn't learned from Toyota was how to consistently develop successful new models that shared common components. Toyota could build five or six vehicles based on the Camry sedan and make money on all of them. GM had been trying to do something similar for a decade, developing cars from a single set of key components that could be sold not only in North America but also overseas by foreign affiliates such as Saab and Opel. Too often it wound up with ungainly cars because design, engineering, and manufacturing weren't using the same playbook. One notable casualty was the midsized Saturn L200. Designed with the same underpinnings as a model from Opel, GM's European affiliate, it had a cramped interior and Spartan design that turned off American customers. It sold poorly from the time it was introduced in 1999 and was discontinued a year ahead of schedule.

The L200 followed earlier flops such as the Opel-based Cadillac Catera sedan and the Chevy-Pontiac-Oldsmobile-Opel minivan. To design a van that would fit on European roads, GM made it narrower than competitors' models. But the minivan never caught on in Europe, and it struggled in the United States, too. Said John

Middlebrook: "If you compromise a vehicle for a specific market—if you compromise the van in terms of width—then you wind up with one that doesn't work that well in either market."

Still in the throes of deploying prepackaged solutions to organizational problems, GM had created APEX (Advanced Portfolio EXploration) as a way to fix product development confusion among its six brands. Fifty new vehicles at a time were to be actively designed, engineered, and test-marketed by a team of more than 120 people. That was too many concepts for anybody to take any of them seriously, and too few people to execute them properly. Once again, GM was using a hammer to kill an ant. APEX was dissolved by the time Bob Lutz arrived in 2001.

Wagoner believed that GM was learning from its mistakes. "What went wrong," he said in 2004, "has to do with everything from organizational mentality and organization structure to how different markets really are and the capability to execute products that can be sold in more than one market. My sense is we've matured in all these areas." He had high hopes for cars like the 2004 Pontiac GTO, which was based on a rear-drive vehicle developed in Australia by GM's Holden affiliate but was powered by a traditional American V-8. Unfortunately, he was overoptimistic. The conservative styling of the Australian GTO offended traditionalists at whom the car was aimed, and production ceased in February 2006. Once again, GM was betting on the come, and once again it would be disappointed.

CHAPTER 12

Succession Battles at Ford

R ed Poling succeeded Don Petersen as chairman and CEO and guided Ford through the recession of 1990–1991. As he got ready to retire in 1993, the board of directors revisited the issue of succession and, once again, passed over Allan Gilmour. I was later told that the Ford family could never accept a gay man as CEO, but the cerebral, witty Gilmour was also perceived to have other shortcomings. His quips made him seem less than authoritative, and his habit of answering a question with another question made him appear indecisive.

In place of Gilmour, a graduate of Harvard College and the University of Michigan's business school, Ford's board of directors chose Alex Trotman to begin as CEO on November 1, 1993. Trotman was a tough-minded Scot whose education had stopped at the high school level and who started work at a Ford plant in Great Britain fetching parts on a bicycle. With his trimmed moustache, fastidious neatness, and military air, Trotman could have played a British colonel in a Merchant-Ivory film. He came by the association honestly, having served four years in the Royal Air Force as a navigator. Trotman had enormous reservoirs of self-confidence. Unlike most CEOs, he could stand alone at a reception without the usual handling by aides, and I once saw him unself-consciously dip a napkin in a water glass to attack a spot on his jacket lapel. His personality was almost totally sublimated in Ford. "When the company does things well, that's my ego trip," said Trotman. "I don't distinguish between myself and the company."

Trotman was affable enough in public, though he would never be accused of being charming. What he did have was stamina. Typically, industry executives are dangled in front of reporters for twenty minutes or so of intensive questioning and then whisked away. On several occasions, I saw the stolid Trotman remain in one place while he answered so many inquiries in such a matter-of-fact manner that reporters eventually wandered off. Trotman had simply worn them out. He also distinguished himself in Michael Moore's satirical film *Roger and Me* by being the only Detroit CEO who would—or could—change the oil in his car on camera.

By the end of his term as CEO in the mid-1990s, Trotman would become better known for his battles with the Ford family, but early on, he pursued the chimera that had eluded Ford CEOs since the 1970s: globalization. Ford had strong operations in North America and in Europe, but they operated as if they were on different planets, thus denying Ford economies of scale. While Toyota was building one Corolla and selling it around the world, Ford was assembling different versions of its models for each side of the Atlantic. Ford had taken its first crack at developing a world car with the 1980 Escort. But by the time development engineers got through modifying the car for their individual markets, the American version and the European version had few parts in common.

For its second attempt in the 1990s, Ford tried something different. It developed a compact sedan called Mondeo for sale in

Europe and then made cosmetic modifications to sell it in North America, where the car was marketed as the 1995 Ford Contour and Mercury Mystique. It was a real learning experience for the company, as I wrote in the June 28, 1993, issue. An indiscreet Ford executive had already conceded that the whole project, code-named CDW27 and including five body styles and new engines and transmissions, would cost six billion dollars, and so Mondeo was forever known as the "six-billion-dollar car." That was twice the money Ford spent on the successful Taurus and Sable, introduced in 1985, and nearly four times as much as it cost Chrysler to bring its 1993 LH cars to market. As a result, Ford stood to make little money on the Mondeo in the United States. Because of intense pricing pressures on small, fuel-efficient cars, it would do well to break even.

As it turned out, the car did worse than that. It lost money, and Ford dropped the U.S. versions after a short run. But that didn't stop Trotman. Ford trucks like the F150 pickup and SUVs like the Explorer had become enormously popular, and the company was flush with cash. So he decided to try his hand at globalization—not with just one car but with the entire company. He called the ambitious project "Ford 2000." Dozens of engineering centers around the world were merged into five new ones, and twenty-five thousand salaried employees were moved to new locations or would report to new bosses. David Lewis, a business historian at the University of Michigan who had written extensively about Ford, called it "the biggest reorganization in the company's history. It is like Columbus setting off on his voyage to India. He found North America, but he might have fallen off the edge."

Ford didn't fall off the edge, but Ford 2000 was not a success. Whole layers of middle management were wiped out, taking with them valuable institutional knowledge. Functionally organized engineering centers meant that local market preferences were too often left out of design and development decisions, and geographic profit centers were eliminated, making oversight difficult. The final blow hit when it came time to develop a second-generation Ford Focus early in the twenty-first century. Europe, a market where small cars were important, went ahead with an all-new version. But North America, where small cars are money losers, decided it couldn't afford an all-new version and proceeded with a modified version of the old first-generation Focus instead. Two entirely different versions of the same car meant no economies of scale.

Trotman was due to retire in 1998, but the speculation had begun several years earlier about who would succeed him. Having wrongly touted Gilmour for several years, I kept my forecasting record at zero by promoting the prospects of a colorless engineer named Edward Hagenlocker. Hagenlocker was considered the father of the hugely successful Explorer and was now running the truck division, Ford's profit machine. I observed that Hagenlocker would make an insurance actuary look high-spirited, and the Ford board apparently agreed, lifting Hagenlocker to the mostly ceremonial post of vice chairman and then easing him out of the company.

I completed my trifecta of bad executive handicapping by touting the prospects of Henry II's son, Edsel, over his nine-year-younger cousin, Bill. I assumed that his age, ambition, and parentage would land Edsel in the CEO job first. Edsel hadn't done well in school, but then neither had his father. And Edsel had some assets: his name resonated with automotive history, he was popular with Ford dealers, and he was a visible figure on Detroit's charity scene. Besides, he'd stuck with the company, working there for twenty-one years while Bill had resigned his job in truck product development and gone off the company payroll, deciding instead to replace his father as chairman of the powerful finance committee of the board of directors.

Working on a story, I was having a difficult time sorting out what all that meant: Would Edsel's perseverance trump Bill's power play? The way Edsel saw it, he was in the lead. "Now you see there are two ladders," he told me. "There is an outside ladder and an inside ladder. But it seems to me that if you are a non-employee, it is hard to be chairman and CEO. You could make Billy chairman of Ford Motor Co. [and] not CEO. Only time is going to tell."

Characteristically, Bill was a bit more diplomatic when discussing competition with his cousin. Said he: "This is a huge company, and there is more than enough room for us both to advance." I got Trotman to weigh in on this topic, too, and when I read between the lines today, I see that he revealed a harder-edged position on the ambitions of both Fords. "Both boys are in prominent positions," he said. "But they agree that any higher position has to be earned. We don't know what happens down the road."

I managed to make up for these past reportorial shortcomings with a story for the October 14, 1996, issue. An analyst tipped me off that Bill was being considered for the job of company chairman (though not CEO) and that Edsel was being sidelined from further promotions. One source wasn't strong enough for a story like this, but *Fortune* managing editor John Huey managed to confirm the story and added some juicy details through an authoritative source of his own. The *Wall Street Journal* was chasing the story, too, which was a problem because we were several days away from getting the magazine to subscribers. To lock in *Fortune*'s exclusive,

Huey leaked it to the *New York Times*, enabling them to publish the story the following day, a Saturday, beating the *Journal* and citing *Fortune* as the source.

Besides disclosing the return of a Ford family member to the head of Ford Motor, the story revealed that Hagenlocker was being eased out and was turning his job over to the fast-rising Jac Nasser. "Nasser bristles with the leadership and decisiveness Hagenlocker lacks," I wrote, "though he's got to get some of the roughness out of him." Edsel, too, had been shunted aside. I quoted a company insider who said that Edsel was not considered to have the brains, drive, or temperament to run the company: "He has all of his father's shortcomings and none of his father's strengths."

Trotman got wind of the story quickly and reportedly became enraged. Said a former Ford executive close to the situation: "Alex was very secretive, and he could get furious about things that appeared in print. He was very angry." I was later told that Trotman tried to kill the story by asking a mutual friend to appeal to Gerald Levin, CEO of Time Warner (parent of *Fortune*'s publisher). When that effort was rebuffed, Trotman began what one insider called "a great witch hunt." He ordered Ford's general counsel John Martin to find out if someone at the company had leaked the story. Ford lawyers, along with attorneys from the company's Washington law firm O'Melveny and Myers, formally interviewed members of the board, including Bill Ford, as well as top executives. They also searched business phone records looking for calls to news organizations.

Several weeks later, Trotman told the board that the investigation had been inconclusive. But feelings were bruised. One director compared the probe to the Nixon White House plumbers' operation that set off Watergate. Bill wouldn't talk about the investigation for the record, but he told friends he found it insulting. Said one: "When you're the owner of the company, this is a highly offensive thing to be quizzed about."

As I later learned, Alex Trotman had more than personal feelings at stake because the board had rejected his succession plan. Apparently, Trotman was intent upon appointing his own successor and, just as intently, wanted to keep the top jobs out of the family's hands. He first proposed Hagenlocker for chairman and CEO and then, when the board demurred, suggested that Hagenlocker and Nasser split the two top jobs. As the deliberations on succession proceeded, said one board member, Trotman "reacted emotionally and not practically." In the fall of 1998 his emotions finally boiled over. When the board of directors approved the promotion of Bill Ford to chairman and Jac Nasser to CEO, Trotman turned to Bill and told him, "Now you have your monarchy back, Prince William."

The man who wasn't there was Gilmour, who, having been twice denied promotion, had retired in early 1995 at age sixty. Since then, he had quietly become involved in charitable activities for gay and lesbian causes, and with a little prodding, he agreed to discuss his career at Ford and his secret life outside the company for *Fortune*.

In an article for the September 8, 1997, issue headlined, "My Life as a Gay Executive," Gilmour told what it was like to be passed over. Like everything else Gilmour did, the story was related with thoughtfulness and feeling. Gilmour said that his ambition had been to become chief financial officer of Ford, and he got the job at the beginning of 1986. During that year he said to both Petersen, who was the chairman, and Poling, who was the president, that he did not wish to have a higher-level job. Said Gilmour: "They had enough people running for higher office, and I thought I could make the best contribution doing the job with it totally in mind. They told me that they'd worry about succession—I didn't need to."

But in the late 1980s, Gilmour had a change of heart; he thought he was the best person to be the next CEO of Ford. In late 1991 or early 1992, he said, Poling had told him he was in fact on track to be the next CEO. Gilmour told me he was worried about his private life, but he figured that being CEO would be a seven-day-a-week job, so it wouldn't be a problem. It was not to be. In July 1992, Gilmour learned that the board had selected Trotman instead. Poling told him that compared with Trotman, Gilmour didn't have broad operating experience. Gilmour asked Poling, "Is there any particular trouble?" And Poling said, "No." Recalled Gilmour: "I'll never know why I was passed over, but I think Red left the succession question to the board and did not take a strong stand. Whether being gay hurt my chances, I honestly don't know. I've heard some people say it did, but I doubt it."

As 1998 went on, the media were awaiting the ascension of Bill Ford to chairman and Jac Nasser to CEO, but in the meantime Trotman's company was tearing up the competition. In 1997, the automaker had made $6.9 billion—the most money, I wrote, of any auto manufacturer, ever. I praised Ford 2000 for having paid off despite doubts and cited as an example the simultaneous development of a new midsized Jaguar, to be known as the S-Type, and the Lincoln LS sedan. The two cars shared key parts of their suspensions and power trains, and because of such moves, the total savings in engineering and development costs from Ford 2000 were projected to run into the hundreds of millions of dollars. It was a good story except for the ending. Both the Lincoln and the Jaguar flopped in the marketplace because they were perceived as compromised vehicles; the Jaguar had too much Lincoln in it, and the Lincoln didn't have enough. The cars were discontinued after a single generation, which was a very expensive solution to a sales problem; cars make the most money after several years, when the cost of development and tooling is paid off.

I also noted that Nasser was demonstrating some fin-de-siècle moves that would become his hallmark. Nasser loved doing the unexpected, and his ideas represented fresh thinking. For instance, he moved the ailing Lincoln-Mercury division from Detroit to Orange County, California, where its managers could rub shoulders with people who drove Toyotas and BMWs instead of Chryslers and Oldsmobiles. But as Nasser began his tenure as CEO in 1999, the country went into recession, the company would take some unexpected hits, and his relationship with Bill Ford would fracture. Those expensive innovations came to look like idiosyncratic indulgences, and that, combined with his inattention to operational details and his abrasive personality, would make Nasser's term at the top a short one.

CHAPTER 13

Wagoner Takes Over

F ord had become a powerhouse, but GM was now a stronger company, too. Tall, broad-shouldered, and steeped in GM lore, Wagoner seemed to me to be a good choice for CEO when he ascended in 2000. And indeed he could claim credit for significant achievements during his time in office. He unified North American operations by abolishing independent fiefdoms, achieved a historic agreement with the United Auto Workers on health care benefits, and aggressively pursued expansion in China. He accomplished all this while winning the affection and loyalty of his subordinates. I never heard a GM'er say a bad word about Wagoner.

But although Wagoner's tenure started well, it ended badly. Initially slow to capitalize on the SUV boom, GM was churning out Tahoes and Suburbans at enormous profit when Wagoner took office. By the time a few years had passed, the market was turning to lighter, more fuel-efficient SUVs built on passenger car platforms called crossovers, and once again, GM lagged behind the industry leaders. Though Wagoner quickly shut down Oldsmobile, GM still lacked the capital to keep Saturn, Pontiac, and Buick uppermost in consumer minds, and the brands faded. He cut costs at a brisk pace, but not quickly enough to offset the pressure on prices brought by foreign competitors and by GM's deteriorating appeal to customers. And mindful of the disruption caused by Roger Smith's 1984 reorganization, Wagoner was too gentle when it came to streamlining GM's still formidable bureaucracy. No executive need fear losing his or her job for anything but the most egregious errors; Wagoner detested ritual hangings.

When the financial crisis of 2008 arrived, Wagoner failed to rise to the occasion. GM's practice of using the most optimistic sales forecasts made him seem out of touch as the market tumbled. The rise in gasoline prices revealed GM's exposure to truck and SUV sales, and Wagoner could deploy no backup plan. Then the credit crunch laid low GMAC Financial Services, making it difficult to finance loans and leases for GM customers. Wagoner's decision to fly to Washington aboard his corporate jet in November made him a poster boy for abusive executive privilege, and his performance before Congress as he went in search of federal aid was unimpressive. After the Treasury Department rejected GM's first viability plan as inadequate, he was finished. In the end, he couldn't escape the fact that during his last four years as CEO, GM had lost eighty-two billion dollars and he couldn't make a convincing argument that the company would turn around. With his resignation at the request of the Treasury Department's auto task force in March 2009, Wagoner would go down in GM history alongside Bob Stempel as a failed CEO.

Wagoner spent sixteen years at or near the top of GM. He was running GM's operations in Brazil in 1992 when Jack Smith made him chief financial offer in the wake of the board coup. Wagoner was thirty-nine and in short order made himself indispensable. He ran global purchasing in addition to finance after Inaki Lopez left for Germany, and 1994, he took over GM's North American operations, its largest revenue center and biggest headache. Looking back, there were signs that Wagoner was too comfortable with the slow progress of change. But as usual, there were enough nuggets of improvement to convince me that he was making real progress.

The more time I spent with Wagoner, the better I liked him. He always struck me as reasonable, and although he could get defensive about criticism, he seldom took it personally. I knew that talking to reporters wasn't his favorite use of time, and I appreciated it when he made an effort. Our relationship started to warm up while he was still serving as head of North American operations. For an article to be published in April 1997, he showed me a part of GM I had never seen before, and it was a revelation — both for what I saw and for the fact that it was Wagoner who showed it to me. There is nothing like a little personal attention from a top executive to win over a journalist.

The part that Wagoner revealed was a couple of rooms in the basement of a building on GM's engineering campus in the industrial suburb of Warren, Michigan. In those windowless spaces were sequestered the data GM used to monitor its competitors and run its business; I called them "GM's secret rooms." One, called the Rigorous Tracking Room, contained a wall chart forty-five feet long that plotted forty-two new vehicle programs — the lifeblood of GM — through their multiyear gestation. The programs were measured for timeliness, quality, and financial performance and color-coded by complexity: a major redesign was tinted maize, while a totally new car was colored blue. Another secret room was dedicated to customer satisfaction. It was filled with charts plotting the direction of classified survey data by model line. Getting all of GM's disparate operations focused on the same objectives was one of the methods Wagoner was using to nudge the company toward Jack Smith's goal to "run common. "

Fascinating as they were, I knew that colored charts were no substitute for decisive action. Wagoner explained why things were moving slowly and, in doing so, displayed some of the patience that GM'ers found so soothing but would later prove to be his undoing. The way Wagoner told it, fixing GM was a multiyear process. "In 1992 and 1993 we were just trying to stop the bleeding," he said. "In 1994 and 1995 we put in some key processes: vehicle development, brand management, running lean. In 1996 and 1997 we are putting in a second round of key processes: engineering productivity, common procedures and systems, and global integration." The payoff, it seemed, was still in the future.

Why was it so hard to get this monster moving? One reason was that despite its size, GM wasn't taking advantage of its economies of scale. Its North American business had grown up as a collection of six separate vehicle makers that were overseen but never really managed. GM operated for years without centralized manufacturing, purchasing, data processing, advertising, or market research. Still used to carving up the market among its own brands (even though that idea was twenty years out of date), GM wasted lots of energy fighting itself. Powerful independent constituencies such as suppliers, dealers, and labor unions benefited from the competition and so encouraged it.

Characteristic of Wagoner's slowness to make fundamental change was his dithering over Oldsmobile. Its sales had skidded from 1.1 million in 1986 to 331,287 in 1996 because the middle of the market, where it competed, was being taken over by stronger brands. GM had discussed linking Olds with Saturn to take advantage of Saturn's strength in customer satisfaction but had decided against it. So it was using "needs segmentation" to find a better way to differentiate Olds from the other divisions. In the past, a GM executive conceded, GM had ignored market research because its engineers thought they knew best. This time, the marketers and brand managers were in charge, but they didn't have any more success carving out exclusive positioning for Olds.

At the time, my opinion on needs segmentation was mixed. The late 1990s Buick Park Avenue and the Pontiac Grand Prix developed under Vince Barabba's system seem perfectly styled to their target customers. But to me, the Chevrolet Malibu and Buick Century looked as if their intended buyers were named Hertz and Avis. Utterly missing from this collection was a car that might stop traffic. Wagoner was a bit defensive. "If you look at how our products have done, not with the buff books and auto writers but with the people they are intended for, we've had a lot of success," he insisted. Years later, GM's product development became the subject of national debate as commentators kept asking the question why GM couldn't build any cars that Americans wanted to buy. The answer was that some of its passenger cars were appealing in a mechanical sort of way, but none was really emotionally compelling.

Wagoner's first tour as head of North American operations ended in 1998, when he was elevated to president and chief operating officer. The fairest grade to give him would be an "incomplete." He kept too many of GM's old-line managers in place and was unable to halt the company's continued slide in market share. GM was slow to take advantage of market changes, costing it billions in net earnings. Wagoner also antagonized dealers when he approved a plan for GM to buy some of them out. That put company-owned dealers into competition with independent ones. Typically reasonable, Wagoner said afterward: "I learned a lot. Having your key constituents mad at you is not the way to be successful."

Wagoner was promoted to CEO in 2000, and by the time I caught up with him again, GM was showing one of its periodic signs of life. Chevy was outselling Ford for the first time in eleven years, and Wagoner had made industry headlines by luring veteran executive Bob Lutz out of semiretirement. The attention-grabbing Lutz was in the papers every day; a lot of CEOs wouldn't stand for that, but it didn't seem to bother Wagoner. For his part, Lutz praised Wagoner as "the most intelligent person I ever worked for." If that was a backhanded compliment (and rereading it in 2009 suggests it could have been), Lutz never displayed any sentiment to the contrary.

With Lutz leading the charge, GM backed away from customer needs segmentation, which while producing vehicles that on paper delivered value, treated cars as transportation devices. In his new position, Lutz put designers in charge of a process that would emphasize the emotional appeal of cars, rather than mechanically checking off the boxes on a marketing punch list. "One critically bad thing at GM has been the subordination of design," Lutz said, with characteristic bluntness. "People who rent our cars at airports look at them and say, 'Isn't this depressing?'" Not all of Lutz's cars were hits, but GM's batting average went way up.

As Wagoner became more comfortable in public, he developed a deft, self-deprecating sense of humor. During a speech about innovation to an engineering association, he acknowledged that "not all of GM's past innovations have come out exactly the way we intended." Then he cited the accident-prone Corvair and the infamous robots at Roger Smith's "factory of the future" in Hamtramck, Michigan. Instead of painting cars passing by on the assembly line, the robots turned their spray guns on each other. Was the recognition of old mistakes another step in GM's recovery? It seemed that way to me.

For all his patient ways, Wagoner could be intensely competitive. In a drive to get back to 30 percent market share, which GM had last seen in 1997, Wagoner juiced up customer incentives like zero percent financing to boost sales. In Detroit staffers were wearing GM lapel pins with the number "29" attached to the bottom, signifying Wagoner's stretch target for the year. Market-share targets had been a big no-no under Wagoner's predecessor Jack Smith, because they recalled past failures when GM would dump cars in rental fleets just to move the metal. Worse, GM would announce that it was going to hit a certain share level and then not be able to deliver. "We got burned a couple of times," admitted Wagoner. "We came out and said, 'We're going to do this'—and didn't make it." But Wagoner was convinced that GM had to grow to live, and he was keeping the pressure on everyone to perform.

But GM got burned this time, too. Wagoner was never able to get back to 29 percent, much less 30 percent, and the company's U.S. market share continued to sink throughout his tenure as CEO. In those heady times, automakers thought that through customer incentives—GM was ladling out almost $2,600 per vehicle— they could eliminate, or at least postpone, one of the auto industry's iron laws. In the past, strong sales years were consistently followed by weak ones—a period known as "payback"—because customers were thought to have a finite need for cars. But by keeping deals generous and flooding the market with new models, GM thought it could make demand cycles obsolete. Alas, it was not to be. After GM approached sales of seventeen million cars and trucks in 2004 and 2005, the onset of a major recession sent sales plummeting to thirteen million in 2008 and down even more to ten million in 2009.

The shrinking market also doomed Wagoner's plan to keep GM big so that the company could cover its fixed costs, such as retirement obligations for pensions and health care. Wagoner was convinced that GM could never save its way to prosperity. "To the extent that we sell more products," he explained, "we amortize those costs over more cars and trucks sold, and the impact [of retiree costs] isn't so great." But like others, this strategy failed, too. GM suffered a double whammy: the market shrank, and so did GM's share.

Wagoner could usually be counted on to observe the industry's unspoken prohibition against criticizing a competitor. One topic that brought out his worst instincts, however, was the Japanese yen and his undying belief that the Japanese government was manipulating its currency to the advantage of Japanese automakers. A weak yen—anything above, say, 115 yen to the dollar—made Japanese cars seem inexpensive (Wagoner would say ridiculously cheap) in the United States. European auto executives also complained about the impact of exchange rates, and Iacocca, in his day, whined about them too, but Wagoner was the worst in recent times. If his jawboning had any impact, it hasn't been recorded. And on those occasions when the yen did strengthen, to GM's advantage, he never credited the currency swing with the company's success.

The fiftieth anniversary of the *Fortune* 500 in April 2004 called for a big GM takeout, and I decided to look at how Wagoner was trying to fix the broken parts of a ninety-five-year-old company. Wagoner was in a reflective mood, and he was again willing to provide an honest evaluation of past events. He pointed to the Roger Smith era as the most damaging in the company's past. "The '80s were probably the toughest decade in GM's history from an automotive perspective," he told me. "The financial results and market share results weren't that bad. But it seems like we lost some of our relative competitive positioning during the decade. We hired a lot of people, and we've been carrying those people since. We've been 12 to 14 years digging out from that."

Neither did he spare himself or his predecessor from criticism. "We didn't do everything right over the last 12 years," he went on. "About three times during that period you think you've got it, and then something else comes up." Wagoner's conclusion: "Don't ever think you've got it licked, because you probably don't" (as later events would demonstrate). It would have been nice to report at this point that under Wagoner's patient direction, GM was delighting customers, dazzling investors, and blowing the doors off the competition. It wasn't. In Europe and South America, it was losing money. In the all-important American market, GM's performance remained a mixed bag. It enjoyed spectacular results with full-sized pickup trucks and SUV derivatives like the Chevy Suburban and the Cadillac Escalade that sold in huge volumes (1.7 million annually) and produced outsized variable profits — as much as fifteen thousand dollars per vehicle. But GM lost money on small cars marketed by Saturn and Chevy, and it shortchanged

Pontiac and Buick, leaving them with outdated lineups. Overall, GM managed to squeeze a profit margin of only 1 percent out of North America in 2003.

That weak performance during a boom year was a harbinger of hard times. The true extent of GM's competitive shortcomings wouldn't become glaring for a year or two, but it should have been a signal to Wagoner that he needed to amp it up. It wasn't, and it became his, and GM's, undoing.

CHAPTER 14

Nasser, Ford, and Mulally

Whatever problems GM was having weren't coming at the hands of its domestic competition. Under Daimler's ownership, Chrysler remained an erratic and essentially vulnerable player. Ford, meanwhile, after the relative stability of the Trotman era, was once again consumed by the palace intrigue that is as much a part of the company as its blue oval trademark.

Ordinarily, the CEO of a company as large and prominent as Ford who was as young (fifty-one) as Jac Nasser and enjoyed his colorful backstory (the son of Lebanese immigrants, he was raised in Australia) would have enjoyed considerable media attention. For his part, Nasser, a small man with a large ego, would have basked in the prominence. But his story couldn't compete with that of the young scion who had maneuvered against entrenched forces to become the chairman of the board of the company that his great-grandfather had founded ninety-six years earlier.

History will record that Bill Ford was not an effective steward of his family's fortunes. His first two and a half years as chairman were consumed by his battles with Nasser. After he took over as CEO in October 2001, things got worse. Subordinates mocked him behind his back and made fun of his environmental beliefs;

he would later complain that they took his directives and "slow walked" them, effectively consigning them to the dustbin. But Ford himself betrayed a lack of direction. His indecision could be seen in the succession of turnaround plans that he announced and his inability to maintain a coherent future product program. He was well-intentioned and sincere and, because of his name, was well liked by Ford employees who took pride in the company's heritage. But the events of the early twenty-first century produced more challenges for the company than he could handle.

It didn't help that Ford surrounded himself with palace courtiers who smoothed over his self-doubts and made this pampered though insecure son of the industrial aristocracy feel accepted and welcome. Their presence only revealed how deficient Ford had become in first-class management talent. In retrospect, Bill Ford's greatest contribution to his family's company was his decision to step aside as CEO and reach outside the company in September 2006 for an engineer from Boeing named Alan Mulally to replace him.

In the beginning, Bill Ford got a royal welcome. He was treated gently by business reporters and the automotive press who were more interested in his life story than his qualifications for the job or ability to do it. *Fortune* was no different. An April 3, 2000, cover story portrayed the new chairman of the board as a New Agey executive with pronounced green leanings who was ready to shake things up. "Roll over, Business Roundtable," began a story by writer Betsy Morris. "Here comes an entirely new old-economy boss. Bill Ford Jr., is an unapologetic environmentalist. . . . He is an iconoclast. . . . He says what he thinks and does what he thinks he should. 'Greenpeace has asked me to speak. I think I'm going to do it,' he mused recently in his office. 'Yeah, why not? Maybe I should wear a flak jacket.'"

But more serious problems were looming. Fifteen months into Ford's tenure as chairman of the board, there were already reports that he and Nasser weren't getting along, and the question *Fortune* raised was whether Ford could handle the conflict. "The rumors are wild: that they had a shouting match in the lobby of the Dearborn Ritz-Carlton, that they had to be separated by security during an argument at world headquarters." GM's Bob Lutz was prescient. "I think it'll be a miracle if they last two years," said Lutz. "One wants to be the hero of the environment. The other wants to be the hero of the shareholders."

Bill was more successful dealing with the ambitions of his cousin, Edsel. He came up with an innovative solution: he and Edsel would stand united on family issues but go their own way with their individual careers. It seemed to work. When Edsel realized that he wasn't going to rise through the company to its top, he quit and served as a five-hundred-thousand-dollar-a-year consultant, mostly on dealer relations. Friends said he was bitterly disappointed not to have advanced higher, but he kept his feelings to himself.

At first, Bill stayed out of the way while Nasser moved aggressively to remake Ford. Nasser contemplated buying Nissan (but relented and allowed Renault to get 30 percent of the company instead) and eventually wound up with Volvo. He also tried to reposition Ford as a consumer products company that stayed connected to its customers after they had purchased an automobile. But he was thrown off stride by the Explorer rollover crisis in 2001. The treads of Firestone tires on Ford Explorer SUVs and some Ranger pickup trucks were peeling off under pressure and causing drivers to lose control and crash. The tires were connected to more than fourteen hundred accidents and other mishaps in the United States involving eighty-eight deaths, and the federal government launched an investigation. The tire problems were happening on Nasser's watch, and he had to solve them. Said a Ford insider at the time: "This is a test of character for Jac. He's been saying we're a consumer-focused company, and the way he handles this will determine his credibility going forward—both internally and externally."

Nasser initially turned down invitations to testify before congressional committees, but public pressure soon forced him to accept. His performance as a spokesman was mixed. Critics have chided him for appearing too stiff and rehearsed on TV; with his formal syntax and thick Australian accent, the CEO came across as an unfortunate combination of Al Gore and Crocodile Dundee.

Nasser was running into other troubles. By the middle of June 2001, I reported, Ford sales were down, recalls and defects were up, and Nasser was on the hot seat. His impersonal, hard-driving style was taking its toll. "We've been trying to improve content and reduce cost at the same time, and it is starting to fracture people psychologically," said one company insider. "We need to get back to continuous improvement rather than trying to invent the wheel with every new program." According to a joke around the company, GE's Jack Welch was surrounded by ten subordinates who would take a bullet for him, whereas Nasser would be surrounded by ten subordinates who wanted to put a bullet in him.

Rumors about Nasser's imminent departure were building, and Ford Motor's top executives worked overtime to stamp out reports of an impending management shakeup. "We've always had camps here," said Bill Ford. "I don't think there is anything I can do or Jac can do to prevent it. The fact is that we have a very easy relationship." Nasser declared in early June 2001 that he had the support of the directors, including Ford, and that no big changes were coming. But the automaker's quality and sales problems appeared to be eroding Nasser's backing, and his organizational structure was suspect. Since becoming CEO in January 1999, Nasser had been running Ford as a one-man show. He had fifteen direct reports but no designated number two. Said Nasser: "We [Bill and I] share the same views about where the company should be heading. We probably should have moved a little earlier than we did [to stop rumors about a clash]. Now it is a question of refocusing our energies on the fundamentals."

There would be no peace. In early October, Bill Ford huddled with family members at their regular yearly meeting in Dearborn. Although he said the outcome was "not predetermined," he gained their support for a move on Nasser. Within days, he decided to act. As he said later, "Our problems continued to mount, the pressure from the outside became enormous, and the internal speculation and the division into opposing camps nearly had us paralyzed."

By the end of the month, Nasser was out as CEO, and Bill Ford replaced him. He had precious little applicable experience, but it was his company, and outside board members would insist— lamely, in retrospect—that he was the best available candidate. The wheels had already come off. Ford had reported $7.2 billion in net income for 1999; in 2000 it lost $5.5 billion, the bulk of which was a onetime charge of $4.1 billion for a rigorous and painful restructuring program. The company said that it would close five plants, lay off thirty-five thousand people—about 10 percent of its workforce—

cut purchasing costs, and sell assets while it tried to refill its product pipeline and improve quality. It would also eliminate four car lines, including the Mercury Cougar and Lincoln Continental.

Though Nasser was mostly at fault for not paying closer attention to operations during the downturn and allowing the rift with his boss to fester, Bill Ford shared some blame. He was probably unrealistic to expect that an executive as driven as Nasser, who fought his way up through the company, would easily share responsibility with somebody who seemed to owe his position to birth. And by actively promoting his own causes, Ford gave the appearance of operating with a higher moral authority than his CEO, who had to make difficult decisions about employee evaluations, plant closings, and layoffs. Said Ford: "Maybe I was naive. Clearly we didn't do everything right."

Every time I looked at Ford, a new crisis seemed to have broken out. As Bill admitted to *Fortune* in 2004: "In those first six months, my head was spinning. I almost wasn't sure where to begin. It was panic stations every day." Infighting became epidemic. A few months after he became CEO, Ford assembled three of his top executives to say, in effect, chill out. He made it clear that he would not allow their individual differences to sink his revitalization plan. Said Ford: "If I hear about backbiting, I kill it right away. I confront it and I won't tolerate it."

He also had to watch his back for dissident members of the Ford family, a problem that surfaced publicly a few years later. The issue was a simple one: their wealth was evaporating on Bill's watch even before the financial crisis of 2008. What would you do, I asked in the April 16, 2007, issue, if $581 million of your family's fortune had been vaporized in just five and a half years? The family's class B stock was valued at $1.14 billion when Bill took over as CEO of Ford Motor in 2001. By spring 2007, the shares were worth less than half that. To make matters worse, the clan's once-lucrative dividend stream had dried up: payouts that amounted to more than $28 million annually as recently as 2005 had been slashed to zero in 2007.

What Ford needed was a professional CEO. Several internal candidates had competed for the prize, but all were found wanting and had left the company, so the logical thing to do was to go outside. "There are some lessons from the past that Bill Ford might find useful," I wrote with rare prescience in 2003. "His uncle Henry Ford II . . . hired the Whiz Kids (including Robert McNamara) and recruited Ernie Breech, a former GM executive, to manage operations and stabilize the company. . . . Bill Ford won't admit as much, but he might do well to find his own Ernie Breech."

Finally, he did. By 2006, Ford Motor, which had seemed so prosperous a few years earlier, was struggling. Before the year was out, it would cut ten thousand more salaried jobs, offer buyouts to all seventy-five thousand of its hourly workers, and still report an annual loss of $12.7 billion, the worst in its 103-year history. So Bill Ford went outside for help. Working without any executive search help, he turned up Boeing executive Alan Mulally. Having been twice passed over as head of the aerospace giant, the ultracompetitive Mulally was ready for a new challenge when Ford convinced him to terminate a thirty-seven-year-career in commercial aviation and come to Ford as CEO.

At our first meeting, Mulally, who had by then only twelve days of on-the-job automotive experience, stressed that he had already identified Ford's basic problems—too much complexity, too little cooperation, not enough transparency—and was moving to fix them. His big idea had been to start a new meeting with his direct reports to review operations called the Business Plan Review. I wasn't impressed. Thinking of myself, after thirty years reporting on the business, as something of an industry insider, I felt put off that an outsider could come in as CEO to a company as complex as Ford and make a positive impact. Besides, Mulally didn't fit my image of what a CEO should be. He had the personality of an Eagle Scout who had memorized *How to Win Friends and Influence People* and dressed like a scoutmaster, invariably in a blue blazer, blue oxford-cloth button-down shirt, and red tie. For months, I thought of Mulally as the "aw, shucks" CEO, because when he was asked a complicated question about the car business, he invariably replied with some disarmingly simple answer.

Once again, my personal reactions would lead me astray. True, Mulally was a neophyte when it came to the car business, but he was highly skilled at managing complex industrial businesses. Here was a man, after all, who had been the chief engineer on the development of the Boeing 777, one of the most successful airplanes of all time. It turned out that another meeting like the Business Plan Review was exactly what Ford needed. Mulally, an engineer's engineer who had aspired to be an astronaut, had spent hours studying Ford and decided that what it lacked was focus and discipline. He used that Thursday meeting to instill both.

I had been seeing signs that Mulally was making progress as Ford avoided the financial meltdown of the two other Detroit companies, but final confirmation didn't come until the end of 2008, when he announced that, unlike GM and Chrysler, Ford would not be requiring any government loans. That decision looked wiser and wiser by the day, as the Obama administration enmeshed itself ever more deeply in the affairs of GM and Chrysler as they went through bankruptcy.

So I began discussions with Ford about preparing a profile of Mulally—and was surprised by the access that I got. Mulally chose to overlook my more uninformed and critical remarks made in articles about both Ford and Boeing, and instead focused on a long article I had written called "GM and Me." The article's tone was more one of sorrow and resignation than it was of criticism or fault-finding, which made it less scolding than others about the auto industry that were appearing at the time. Mulally had liked the article, and that set the stage for what came next.

When I arrived in Dearborn in March 2009, not knowing what to expect, I was informed that instead of having the brief interview with Mulally I expected, I would be spending two-and-a-half hours with him—and what a two-and-a-half hours it was. Mulally had prepared for the interview as if he was cramming for a final exam and had compiled a thick loose-leaf binder containing my previous stories as well as his analysis about what Ford needed. One page, a complex hand-drawn diagram that summarized his goals for Ford, headlined "The Plan," was reproduced in the magazine. In addition, he showed me five more binders filled with annotated material he'd compiled on taking the Ford job.

Seating himself next to me at a conference table in his office, Mulally took me through the binder page by page, not moving on until I nodded or otherwise signaled agreement. Mulally was absolutely confident in his vision for Ford—a globally unified company focused on the Ford brand—and he wouldn't back off until he had gotten me on board with him. He didn't let up until he had turned all my "nos" and "maybes" into "yesses."

I came away with a new appreciation for the value of energy—Mulally was working twelve-plus hours a day—confidence, and persistence. Mulally had enjoyed enough success in his life so that winning over others to his side came as second nature. In addition, he was so competitive—Mulally is a crack tennis player and golfer—that he did not want to quit until he had won. He was convinced that his analysis showed him where Ford should be heading, and he was determined to get it there.

By the time our meeting was over, Mulally had worn me out. I can't imagine how his Ford subordinates—most of whom are competitive and successful in their right—put up with him each day, except that his optimism is contagious and makes you want to be part of his team. Mulally's lasting legacy at Ford, assuming he can restore it to financial health, may be that he can unify the management and subdue the infighting that has embroiled the company in the past. His choice of a successor will say a lot about his impact.

At the end of 2009, Ford was showing signs of recovery, but big tests awaited in 2010. In one of his first moves, Mulally had ordered that two small cars sold in Europe, the Focus and the Fiesta, be adapted for North American sale as well. That decision carried with it two big risks: one, that Americans would begin to gravitate toward smaller cars, whether for reasons of higher fuel prices, concern about climate change, or fashion; and two, that they would stop equating small cars with cheap cars and be willing to pay higher prices for more handsomely equipped models with European pedigrees.

If those bets pay off and the market recovers, then Mulally's decision to reject federal aid for Ford will be vindicated. The company still controlled by its founding family will thus be able to conduct its business unencumbered by the government (in GM's case) or controlled by a foreign partner (in Chrysler's). Mulally can then move back to Seattle, secure in his place in history next to Ernie Breech as another outsider who helped save Ford.

CHAPTER 15

The Legend of Lutz

The history of GM, Ford, Chrysler, and nearly every auto company revolves around the CEO. Running an auto company requires developing strategic goals, investing large amounts of capital, and being willing to place big bets, and only the CEO is in a position to make those decisions. Lesser executives surface from time to time—Ed Cole, father of the Corvair; John DeLorean, the inspiration behind the Pontiac GTO; brand marketing's Ron Zarella—but their appearances are brief and the arc of their careers is short when compared to that of the CEO.

Yet the name of one non-CEO appears again and again in this Detroit history. He is the only executive who had a prominent role at each of the Big Three. And he is one of the few whose reputation has improved over time and seems likely to keep growing. Which leads to an obvious question: If Bob Lutz was so good, why wasn't he a CEO?

Much of Lutz's prominence and success springs from the Lutz persona, which in my experience is remarkable and unique for any industry. The auto business attracts more than its share of over-achievers in sales, marketing, and engineering, and I've encountered dozens of them. The most impressive are the higher-level vehicle engineers, who tend to be trim, fit, well-groomed, disciplined, extremely knowledgeable, and very well spoken. The best radiate competence and confidence and have a star quality about them.

Even among these type A personalities, Bob Lutz stands out like a redwood among saplings. First, there is the physical Lutz. He stands several inches over six feet tall, has a thick shock of white hair, and has a face best described as rugged, with a nose that looks as if it has been broken at least once and uneven teeth. The entire effect is multiplied by Lutz's military bearing—like a U.S. Marine, which he was, standing at attention—and his physique. Lutz has the body of a gymnast, with a well-developed chest tapering into an almost unnaturally small waist. Lutz is so well proportioned that I often suspected him of wearing an elastic vest under his suit. When I saw him in 2009, he was seventy-seven years old and about to retire from GM (like his earlier retirements, it turned out to be temporary). Yet he seemed not to have aged for fifteen years. His face had not begun to sag, and despite a recent back operation, his posture didn't waver.

After the physical Lutz comes the Lutz biography. The word "übermale" doesn't begin to describe it. Taught in the Marine Corps to fly jet trainers, Lutz remained a pilot well into his seventies. He flew a helicopter that he used to commute to work and owned a Czech jet trainer that he took out on weekends. (Lutz never minded being photographed in a flight suit with a helmet under his arm.) As befits an auto executive, Lutz also possessed a moderately sized collection of cars and motorcycles, which included more European models and exotics than the usual Detroit executive would park in his garage. The only time I drove with him, he maneuvered a stock Chrysler sedan briskly through expressway traffic with a police radar detector affixed to the windshield.

Lutz also radiated a distinct personal style. His suits were custom-made, some on Savile Row, to show off his physique and featured sporty twin vents. Likewise, his shirts were made with unusually high collars and worn either tabbed or with a collar pin. Instead of the ubiquitous gold Rolexes so popular in the engineering fraternity, Lutz favored a sportier TAG Heuer watch years before Tiger Woods made it popular, as well as a Breitling. A long cigar (Cuban, I assume) completed the picture. It was brandished unlit in places where smoking was not permitted and enjoyed with relish in places where it was. An attractive, capable younger blonde wife (his third) completed the picture.

Favored with exceptional physical equipment and a psyche that allowed him to give it full expression, Lutz became the center of attention wherever he went in automotive circles. It was a role that he enjoyed and played to the hilt. Although fluent in several European languages, he spoke pungent, unaccented English and was accustomed to dominating conversations. He had the skills of a practiced raconteur and seemed to have a story or anecdote told in his distinctive gravelly voice to fit every occasion. He chose his words with great care and was something of a phrase-maker. It was Lutz, while working at Chrysler, who referred to an early dent-resistant but overweight GM minivan as "the plastic pachyderm," and coined the description "angry kitchen appliance" to describe the benighted Pontiac Aztek. The downside was that a long lunch or dinner with Lutz could leave you with the sense that the air had been sucked out of the room since he was often the only person talking and his cadence was very measured.

The relationship between Lutz and the journalists who covered him was a longtime romance that Lutz cleverly exploited and in which the appeal never faded. He pretended we were equal partners in his five-star world of fast cars and international travel and kept us titillated with high-level gossip. Since we were all eager to be admitted to the Lutz club, his frequent admonitions on dispensing a particularly tasty morsel to "protect me on this" or "don't let this come from me" were always honored. The C-suite insights, confidential information, and sarcastic observations had no equal as information or entertainment. Even public relations executive Steve Harris, who had sat in on hundreds of Lutz interviews at both Chrysler and GM, said he never failed to hear something new and interesting from him.

Born in Switzerland to a banker father, Lutz had a prolonged adolescence and spent four years in the marines before entering college. He graduated from the University of California at twenty-six with a degree in industrial management, and two years later got his MBA. Lutz moved around a lot for an auto guy. Judging from his behavior later on when I knew him, his job changes had something to do with his inclination to speak too candidly. Lutz spent the first eight years of his career at GM Europe and then the next three at BMW. In 1974, he launched what would turn out to be a twelve-year stint at Ford, culminating in posts as chairman of Ford of Europe, head of international operations, and chief of truck operations. But never in doubt about his own abilities and opinions, he clashed with Ford's top management. The Lutz version had him upholding the role of right-brain emotion and style in car development against the narrow-minded, numbers-driven, left-brain bean counters. The Ford version has not been made public.

In 1986, Iacocca recruited Lutz to Chrysler and eventually made him president. Chrysler was heading into one of its periodic swoons, so Lutz championed the Viper sports car to symbolize the company's vitality and then oversaw Chrysler's product renaissance in the early 1990s. But Lutz had a falling out with Iacocca, who had a need for approval and success just as Lutz did but whose insecurities were closer to the surface. Iacocca's taste in cars was aging along with him, and Lutz gossiped about him behind his back, once memorably referring to him as a "doddering old fart." Word got back to Iacocca, and Lutz's chance to succeed him as CEO when Iacocca retired in 1992 was dead.

Lutz stayed on at Chrysler after Bob Eaton arrived, but the "Bob and Bob show" soured, and Lutz retired in 1998 just months before Chrysler merged with Daimler. It was lost on few that Lutz was the only top Chrysler executive who spoke German, and his departure could have been a harbinger for the future of the misbegotten merger. Daimler's Jürgen Schrempp continued to call on Lutz for advice, but he was semiretired and seemingly out of the auto manufacturing business for good when Rick Wagoner recruited him to GM in 2001.

The circumstances of my first meeting with Lutz say a lot about his skill in press relations. In 1989 I had negotiated with Chrysler's public relations team to shadow Lutz for two days to find out what a top auto executive did with his time. Chrysler was then about to launch its second Iacocca-led turnaround with the first Jeep Grand Cherokee, and Lutz, as head of product development, was plenty busy. As a side project, he was spearheading his pet project: the realization of the V-10- powered Viper.

Accordingly, I appeared at a Viper development meeting at Chrysler's old Highland Park headquarters for an eight o'clock meeting on a Monday morning with a photographer to follow Lutz in action. Every meeting I was to attend for the next two days would normally have been off-limits to the press, and any coverage would have had to be accompanied by blood oaths not to reveal confidential information. Lutz could have cared less about such formalities and waved me into the room. Although he didn't know me, his only admonition was along the line of "just don't write anything that will get me into trouble."

With that brief caveat, I followed Lutz for the next forty-eight hours as he toured a design studio, reviewed advertising campaigns, analyzed potential joint ventures, and held performance reviews for his direct reports. It was a remarkable performance—Lutz was candid and seemingly held little back—and well illustrated with photographs taken at each interval. Lutz was pleased with the published results and kept track of the foreign magazines that reprinted the story.

That kind of admiring article is sometimes referred to as a "beat sweetener" that builds a relationship with an important secret. Though I hadn't thought that far ahead, I would like to report that I became fast friends with Lutz. But I failed to invest in the relationship. For one thing, I was intimidated by his über-ness. For another, I found his need for attention to be exhausting at times; there could be only one voice in a room Bob Lutz inhabited. And finally, hordes of other writers were enamored of Lutz; I didn't want to get in line, and I didn't want to become part of the claque.

I did take away one piece of learning from Lutz that was to become essential to my understanding of the industry: even in good times, car companies build and sell cars that are chronic money losers. The reasons are varied: currency swings make cars built overseas unprofitable; competitive or regulatory pressures force manufacturers to sell below cost; larger strategic questions, such as the need to spread overhead, are deemed more important than profitability. Chrysler imported cars made by Japan's Mitsubishi and lost money on them. So did a group of sport coupes it made at home because of low volume. GM lost money on the Pontiac Vibe because it was built in a high-cost California plant. In contrast, some of the least recognized vehicles were the most profitable. Perhaps the biggest moneymaker of all, Lutz confided, was the homely commercial van. The boxy styling seldom needed updating, so it enjoyed long model runs, and there was no import competition.

At GM, Lutz filled an organizational vacuum with a strong personality and a distinct point of view. Whatever product development system was responsible for GM's success in the 1950s had long since atrophied, and Band-Aid solutions like needs segmentation provided only mechanistic solutions to emotional problems: creating cars that people wanted to buy. The demands of too many brands and too few resources drained the effort, as did clashes among product development, finance, and manufacturing over money and methods. GM never seemed to know what it wanted until it saw the research, and then warring factions would clash over what the data meant and where the money should be invested.

One of Lutz's greatest contributions at GM was to prevent mistakes like the Pontiac Aztek, where the germ of a good idea was destroyed by an inability to integrate colliding interests. The Aztek symbolized the failure of a system. GM was producing compromised vehicles because of pressure to meet internal targets for cost and timing and to reuse parts from other programs. Consumer clinics were producing unreliable data that were then twisted to support predetermined conclusions. Design was disenfranchised by being made subordinate to manufacturing, engineering, and marketing.

On Lutz's watch from 2001 to 2009, there were no disasters, though there were fewer smash hits than he would have liked. Possessed of unerring regard for his own good taste, he served as a one-man focus group. Early on, Lutz killed a seven-passenger version of the Saturn Vue that he described as "absolutely grotesque." According to *Automotive News,* a company edict had been issued in the wake of Chrysler's successful Dodge Durango that all crossovers and SUVs be equipped with three rows of seats. Lutz immediately recognized that the increased carrying space could destroy the proportions and performance of the vehicle. He also ordered a redesign of an upcoming Cadillac STS that had a flat roof because GM was trying to save money by reusing the sunroof from the old model. Lutz knew when it was important to spend a few extra bucks on a vehicle.

If Lutz had a fault in product development, it was that he too often steered his efforts toward enthusiasts like himself, cars with flashy designs, sporty pretensions, and high horsepower. Other times, he reached too far in order to make an impact; the Pontiac Solstice he produced shortly after arriving at GM was noticeably inferior in luggage space and in its hard-to-operate convertible top to the Mazda Miata, the longtime leader in the segment. Coworkers complained that he had blind spots, such as disliking the use of natural wood in interiors, and repeated the same stylistic tics. He also tended to be too optimistic about the sales prospects of his favorite creations. Wagoner once joked to me that he had to divide Lutz's volume projections by ten to get a realistic number (Lutz relayed his displeasure when the comment wound up in print).

The first batch of Lutz-inspired models—the Pontiac G6 and Solstice, the Buick LaCrosse—failed to excite buyers. But the second wave that he had a more active role in—the Chevy Malibu, Cadillac CTS, Buick Enclave—have been widely praised by analysts and well accepted by customers. Still, they represented only a fraction of GM's prebankruptcy seventy-plus separate nameplates, and as truck sales began to slip, the company's weakness in passenger cars and middle-market brands was exposed. For years, GM never had the resources to keep all its brands and model lines up to date. The mismatch between market coverage and capital spending wasn't addressed until GM emerged from bankruptcy in the summer of 2009.

Based on his history, you wouldn't have expected Lutz to last at GM. He was the antithesis of the nonconfrontational GM executive and seemed more in the mold of a John DeLorean than a Rick Wagoner. But he managed to achieve progress at GM without making so many waves that his influence was affected. The only complaint I heard in eight years was from an executive whom Lutz displaced, complaining about Lutz's tendency to act like automotive royalty. As he grew older and more secure in his position, he made remarks in public that were less than politically correct, such as at first dismissing Toyota's hybrid cars and denying that global warming was a problem. But their impact was limited. Wagoner would express displeasure about such comments, and public relations operatives would have to explain that it was just "Bob being Bob" and they would be forgotten.

Lutz also had the self-confidence to say the obvious and to correct himself when he misspoke. Just as GM was entering bankruptcy, it was Lutz who pointed out that many of GM's problems were self-inflicted, such as relying on fleet sales, not addressing health care, pension, and other legacy costs, and allowing vehicle design to take a backseat. He added that for decades, GM built inferior vehicles that Lutz called "brilliantly executed mediocrity." Nobody could argue.

I was getting ready to write Lutz's epitaph as an active executive in February 2009 when he announced that he was retiring as product development chief. Shortly after GM entered bankruptcy in June, he promptly unretired and took a job as head of marketing and communications. It would have been fun to see him in action again, but he never got the chance. The dismissal of Fritz Henderson and the arrival of Ed Whitacre was followed by Lutz's reassignment as a "senior advisor" to the CEO. It looked like an anticlimactic end to a career that is likely never to be duplicated.

CHAPTER 16

The Uneven Legacy of Lee

After he retired from Chrysler, Lee Iacocca couldn't get out of Michigan fast enough. He immediately packed up and headed for California. Iacocca chafed at being away from the action, however, and over the next fifteen years, he got involved in a series of high-profile business deals, nearly all of which turned out badly. Still, he persisted; he couldn't resist the opportunity to make a buck. As recently as 2009, he was in the news again at the age of eighty-four promoting "Iacocca edition" fortieth-anniversary Mustangs. There was nobody like Iacocca.

Even in retirement, Iacocca remained a fascinating personality because of his unique insights, pungent expressions, and willingness to be politically incorrect. As far as managing editor Marshall Loeb was concerned, there was no such thing as too much Iacocca in *Fortune*, and he turned up on the cover again of the May 30, 1994, issue. The hook this time was the success of the Chrysler minivan that Iacocca had championed a decade earlier. I had no problem with the concept: getting an assignment from the managing editor meant that there would be little difficulty getting the story in the magazine once I had written it. And unlike nearly all of my colleagues in the automotive press, I liked minivans. With their high-mounted captain's chairs and armrests, they were easy to drive and extremely comfortable on long trips. As the parent of two small children, Alexander and Maddie, then aged ten and seven, I also saw the value of having two rows of backseats so that each could have his or her own space.

To interview Iacocca, I flew out to his house in a gated community south of Palm Springs in southern California. The interview took place in a comfortable den adjacent to the living room, and Iacocca squeezed in the time before he headed out for a golf lesson. The one discordant note was provided by his third wife, Darrien Earle. She never made a physical appearance, but I couldn't help but overhear her as she shouted instructions to Iacocca through her closed bedroom door. I made a mental note: this doesn't bode well for the future. (Married in 1991, the couple separated shortly after my visit. Earle accused Iacocca of spying on her, making her a prisoner in her home, and spreading word that she was an adulteress. Their divorce agreement contained a provision that neither speak ill of the other.)

The minivan story provided another excuse for a verbatim Q&A with Iacocca. His musings this time on retirement and current affairs were mostly ephemeral, except for a riff on Bill and Hillary Clinton. Iacocca was a vocal backer of the North American Free Trade Alliance, which President Clinton was pushing, and was offered a night in the White House Lincoln bedroom in recognition of his support. Iacocca appreciated the Clintons' hospitality, he said, but wasn't sold on the "two-for-the-price-of-one" business. "I have nothing against Hillary Clinton. She was very nice to me that night. She showed me to the Lincoln Room. She didn't tuck me in, but she saw me to the room and wanted to talk a little bit about health care." Iacocca's bottom line: "A very smart woman, very engaging. But I've lived long enough to know that if my wife were in Chrysler meetings, everybody would have played to her."

Outside the pages of *Fortune*, other writers were exposing Iacocca's less appealing qualities. They found plenty. Doron Levin of the *New York Times* in *Behind the Wheel at Chrysler* wrote that "students of dysfunctional management will savor the descriptions of Iacocca's executive style. They include, but are not limited to, cronyism, personal vendettas, strategic blunders, impulsive decision-making, and just plain bad judgment." In truth, Iacocca was afflicted by lots of ideas, many of them bad. They included diversifying Chrysler into finance and high technology, lavishing hundreds of millions of dollars on a stillborn sports car project, and buying back Chrysler stock at twenty-two dollars before reissuing it at ten dollars.

It was all true, but it was also part of Iacocca's genius. He always had his eye on the next big thing, and it was the job of his board of directors and his subordinates to help him sort out the good ideas from the less good ones. This was a man who invented three hugely successful product segments and renovated a fourth: sporty cars (Mustang), minivans (Dodge Caravan and Plymouth Voyager), sport-utility vehicles (Jeep), and convertibles (Chrysler Le-Baron). I can't think of any other executive who is associated with even one new segment.

Iacocca's greatest failing was his weakness for material pleasures. Levin quotes one executive's estimate that Chrysler employed some twenty-five people "exclusively for the care, feeding, and personal whims" of the chairman. Besides the pilots and attendants on the executive jet, there were "security guards, masseurs, drivers, and others . . . who did little but run errands, throw parties, check menus, and make sure the chairman was happy." Like the queen of England, Iacocca traveled without money and counted on aides to pick up the check. Levin portrayed a man who was almost comically self-absorbed and Midas-like in his greed. As Chrysler chairman, Iacocca expended considerable energy chivvying pay increases and other emoluments out of the board, and he once threatened to sue unless they sweetened his pension.

In retirement, Iacocca owned a house in Bel Air, the Palm Springs condo, and a villa in Italy. As a Chrysler retiree he was pulling down half a million dollars a year in consulting fees, had access to the company airplanes, and had joined the boards of companies run by Kirk Kerkorian and Ron Perelman. It wasn't that he needed the money: Iacocca owned forty-two million dollars in Chrysler stock. But he wanted more, and he was fascinated by Kerkorian. Too fascinated, as it turned out, and the man who saved Chrysler in 1980 became a pariah at the company fifteen years later.

Kerkorian and Iacocca became pals in 1990 after Kerkorian made his first investment in Chrysler. As Chrysler's board pushed Iacocca toward retirement in 1992, Kerkorian began to act like the big shareholder he was. That August he formally requested a meeting with the board to discuss Eaton's ascension. Afterward he declared himself satisfied that the interests of shareholders would be represented by the new management, and he withdrew his request for representation on the board. Six months later he purchased another four million shares.

Now that he owned all that stock, Kerkorian went looking for a way to make some money from it. He decided that Chrysler was harboring too much cash on its balance sheet and looked to redistribute some of it to shareholders. Since Iacocca was a big shareholder, he thought that was a good idea, too. So he joined the unsolicited tender offer that Kerkorian launched in 1995 for the rest of Chrysler stock. Iacocca declared that he had no interest in "actively participating in management," a prospect that Chrysler's current managers found as laughable as they found Iacocca's participation offensive. Said Robert S. Miller, former vice chairman of Chrysler and later a corporate restructuring expert: "Lee is not the retiring type. If he has the opportunity to be influential in the core decisions of the company, he'll enjoy that."

The Kerkorian deal failed, and he temporarily faded from the spotlight, but Iacocca didn't. His inability to gracefully step back from an active role in business and his tendency to commit his mistakes in public created a natural headline for my next installment in the psychological portrait of this fascinating man in *Fortune*: "How I Flunked Retirement."

I laid out the premise for the 1996 story in my introduction: Had any CEO suffered more damage to his reputation in retirement than Lee Iacocca? Since he had left Chrysler in 1992, he had been vilified as a hypocrite and a traitor, and publicly castigated for his egotism and greed. Most embarrassingly of all, Iacocca had to sue his former employer to get it to honor his stock options. Chrysler accused Iacocca of illegally disclosing confidential information to Kerkorian, making disparaging statements about the company and its products, and conducting himself in a manner adverse to Chrysler. In sum, the lawyers charged, "Iacocca has acted willfully, wantonly, maliciously, and outrageously to injure Chrysler." Iacocca got his money—twenty-one million dollars—

but he badly bruised his reputation. Word leaked out that Chrysler's new, fifteen-story headquarters building in suburban Auburn Hills, Michigan, outside Detroit, would not be named after Iacocca as planned.

That was all quite a comedown for a guy who besides his achievements at Chrysler wrote one of the best-selling business books of all time, starred in his own TV commercials, raised the money to renovate the Statue of Liberty, and nearly managed to orchestrate a movement to draft himself as a presidential candidate. Was he, in fact, the worst traitor since Benedict Arnold for participating in Kerkorian's abortive buyout bid for Chrysler? Or was there another explanation, one that he hadn't been able to make until now?

Despite the chaos he created for himself, I observed when I met him at his Bel Air home that the old guy looked pretty good. Although he complained that stress had taken several years off his life, Iacocca, at seventy-one, was fit and relaxed. Skin treatments had erased lines in his forehead, and he had replaced his clunky aviator-style glasses with modish round frames. He posed for the cover portrait outside with an expensive sport coat slung over his shoulder. His home, a seven-iron from the Hotel Bel-Air, included a swimming pool, tennis court, four-car garage, and gated driveway. Immaculately decorated, it had a den filled with magazine covers featuring you know who and an upstairs hall lined with celebrity photographs. There was also a bathroom the size of a squash court with a giant whirlpool tub, an oversize shower stall, and a fireplace. Constructed for his ex-wife, it was unused.

As usual, Iacocca dished up an irresistible combination of bravado, gossip, and "who me?" injured innocence. The Kerkorian

Chrysler deal, he declared, was a fiasco, and the publicity backlash startled him. "I was stunned. It was hurtful. And I must confess to you, it shortened my life a little bit." True to form, he blamed Kerkorian for managing it badly. "Kerkorian complained that he got bad press. But he wouldn't talk to anybody. I told him, 'You're not accessible; you're Howard Hughes reincarnated.'"

Yet for a man who valued loyalty, Iacocca seemed oddly oblivious to the impression he created as a former chairman and CEO staging a raid on his own company. And the constant disputes over salary, benefits, and options suggested that, for all his protestations to the contrary, money was very important to him.

Iacocca said that, like most CEOs, he wasn't ready for retirement. He complained that his life had been so structured when he ran the company that he had become isolated. He never talked with the people who made the cars or bought them or serviced them. Moving to California had been a problem, too. "I get lost out here, I really do. Get me off the freeways and I'm dead. . . . If I were to give somebody advice, it would be to hang on to something familiar: at least your house and your wife. . . . I was so dumb I thought I could save my marriage by buying a great house in a nice section of California. The adage about how you can't buy happiness is true."

His West Coast ways were unsatisfying. "I look at my friends and they're all new. Which is good because I like new friends, but I miss so many of my old friends." In fact, Iacocca found there was a lot he didn't like about southern California. "The social life out here isn't much, either. If you go to somebody's house for dinner, everybody looks at each other's clothes. Then you sit down. No, you don't sit down, you have a buffet; you eat standing up. There are a lot of guys you never heard of with these young girls, and it's show-time. After you eat, you go in to see a movie. . . . Instantly, when the movie is over, everybody gets up to shake hands, trade a little gossip, get in their cars, and go home. Why not just go to the movies?"

Here was a man who had accomplished extraordinary things in business, media, and politics, yet he could still feel sorry for himself—and do so publicly in the pages of a national magazine. "You can plan everything in life, and then the roof caves in on you because you haven't done enough thinking about who you are and what you should do with the rest of your life. Those guys who retire at 53 with early buyouts have a hell of a problem."

It was a remarkable performance, and I can't recall a business-person of comparable stature laying his psyche bare with such di-rectness. I felt like an analyst, with Iacocca as my patient. Yet I worried that his appeal to *Fortune* readers might be getting stale. At each of our meetings, I wondered if I'd seen the last of Lee. He was repeating some of the old stories, and I wondered how many times he could keep reinventing himself.

Several more times, as it turned out. I was the third wheel at an uncomfortable lunch at the Bel Air house a few years later with another retired auto CEO, GM's Bob Stempel. Iacocca was in-volved with a company that made battery-powered bicycles—he had a weakness for unorthodox business ventures—and Stempel was running a company that made batteries. I hadn't written sym-pathetically about Stempel, so our relationship was awkward, but it didn't matter. Both of us sat back and allowed Iacocca to domi-nate the occasion, the way he always did.

Iacocca kept threatening to write another book, and he finally did in 2007, so I found myself out in Bel Air again doing a piece for the magazine and a video for our web site, CNN/Money.com. A CNN camera crew with all its equipment had taken over Iacocca's library, and we were perched on high-mounted black canvas director's chairs to tape the interview. Both of us were uncomfortable. We were used to more intimate conversations, and Iacocca, by then eighty-two, didn't like all the clutter in his house and didn't adapt quickly to new situations.

Still, he had learned his lines. Daimler had just put Chrysler up for sale, and Iacocca was ready to jump into the fray, declaring his willingness to make a bid for the company. "If I had the money," he said. "I'd come out of retirement to buy it. Chrysler builds great cars. Maybe you could sell off Jeep, but I would hate to see it busted up. [Anyway] I've done my time in Detroit. I live in L.A. now. [Former Daimler Chrysler chairman] Jürgen Schrempp asked me to come work for him, and I said, 'Where do I have to live?' When he said, 'Stuttgart,' I said, 'Forget it.'"

As long as Chrysler remained in the news, a quotation from Iacocca seemed to be essential. So as the company slid toward bankruptcy in 2009, journalists jockeyed to get an observation or two from the old man. I was not among them. The past stories we'd done had been so much fun that I didn't want to spoil the memory by grabbing quotes over the phone. Besides, I rationalized, doesn't the authority of a commentator diminish at some remove from the events he is commenting on? Iacocca had been retired for fifteen years. And at eighty-four, he certainly deserved to be left alone.

Unless he went out and stirred things up on his own again. In which case, I'd be on the next plane to California.

CHAPTER 17

GM's Inevitable Collapse

I n retrospect, 2005 should have been seen as the year when the GM warning flags came out. It was now becoming clear that whatever Wagoner did, the company was headed off a cliff. It was a year when the board of directors should have stepped in and demanded more action than Wagoner was taking. They did not. Ford and Chrysler were on the cusp of big changes, but at GM it was still "steady as she goes."

The first quarter of 2005 was like a slow-motion car wreck. Buyers stopped responding to GM's offerings even as the company's incentives neared the four-thousand-dollar level. Sales of high-profit SUVs like the Chevrolet Suburban tumbled in the face of then-expensive fifty-five-dollar-per-barrel oil and more modern vehicles from rivals. And GM's lovingly nurtured and heavily marketed new models—the Pontiac G6, Buick LaCrosse, and Chevy Cobalt—turned out to be too timid to excite consumers. Bob Lutz hadn't had enough time to sprinkle his magic dust.

For several weeks that year, GM executives tried to put the best gloss on events, grabbing at bits of encouraging news when sales showed glimmers of improvement. But when results were tallied in early March it was clear that the company's North American operations, which provided nearly two-thirds of its automotive revenue, were hitting a wall. Unsold cars had piled up on dealers' lots and market share had slid to 24.4 percent, down three full points from a year earlier. GM tried to pull out of the skid by slashing prices on some midsized SUVs and reassigning a top executive to revamp its sales strategy. It wasn't enough. "The New Cars Aren't Hits" blared a page 1 headline in *Automotive News* in early March.

Belatedly, Wagoner began to move, announcing changes in an early morning conference call with investors and journalists on March 16. Sounding chagrined yet resolute, he announced that sales in 2005 were running far below what GM had forecast and that it wouldn't be able to achieve the earnings targets it had provided Wall Street only two months earlier. Instead of breaking even for the first quarter, GM now expected to lose $850 million. For the full year, it forecast that earnings would be as much as 80 percent lower than previously indicated. Cash flow, a closely watched measure at a capital-intensive company like GM, was hurting, too. It would swing from $2 billion positive to $2 billion negative.

The scary news crushed GM's stock, which lost $4.71 a share that day, falling to $29.01. In ten months, GM had lost fully 40 percent of its market capitalization—motorcycle maker Harley-Davidson was now worth more. Analysts pulled out old stock charts to discover that GM shares were selling for twenty dollars less on a split-adjusted basis than they were in 1965. Credit agencies immediately reviewed GM's bond rating. Another downgrade by Standard and Poor's would push GM below investment grade, sharply raising its borrowing costs and making its auto loans more expensive than those of its competitors.

Wagoner's announcement reinforced the impression that GM's forty-year decline in North America was not just continuing but accelerating. It created a picture of a helpless giant that didn't know its business well enough to forecast results with any accuracy. And in this era of shaky CEO tenure, it also raised questions about the longevity of Wagoner and his team.

The reasons behind GM's fall were clear. Rivals like Toyota and Hyundai were moving faster, and past mistakes had left deep dents in GM's brands. The dream team Wagoner assembled by hiring retired Ford executive John Devine as chief financial officer along with Lutz had failed to produce the expected revival. Cadillac's notable success after a multibillion-dollar investment was overshadowed by big declines in GM's other brands. (How long had it been since a neighborhood teenage boy aspired to own a pavement-ripping Pontiac or his father a comfortable Buick?) And bad as the first-quarter sales figures were, they understated the degree to which consumers increasingly shopped elsewhere. Analyst Steve Girsky of Morgan Stanley (who later would go to work at GM advising Wagoner and then, in 2009, be named the union representative on the board of the new GM) estimated that low- or no-profit sales to GM employees, relatives, retirees, and suppliers, as well as to fleet buyers, accounted for nearly one-third of the company's car sales. So the true appeal of GM's brands was vastly overstated.

Wagoner's strategy didn't leave him much room for error. In arguing that GM needed to get bigger, not smaller, to support its enormous fixed costs, he had taken off the table any discussion of slimming the company by eliminating brands or product lines.

Meanwhile, he chipped away at GM's cost structure and rode the attrition curve of its workforce by allowing people to retire without replacing them. Wagoner figured that if GM could survive for the next few years, the number of living retirees would start to decline—reducing the company's pension and health care obligations—and the overall market would grow sufficiently to boost both revenues and profits. Longer term, Wagoner was counting on a rise in the number of licensed drivers over the next decade to lift the size of the industry and GM along with it.

You could have called it Wagoner's "wait-and-see" strategy. Still, I offered the opinion that Wagoner's job seemed safe. I complained again that his biggest shortcoming was his inability or unwillingness to make the grand public gesture—a deal with the UAW, a visible firing, a technological breakthrough—that would galvanize the company and capture the public's imagination. But if GM were easy to fix, I concluded, the job would have already been done by now.

Wagoner did decide to make a medium-sized gesture by reclaiming his old job as head of North America while retaining his responsibilities of chief executive officer and chairman of the board. It was an impressive example, I thought, of the coach sending himself into the game when it was on the line. His competitive juices were flowing, and he wasn't giving up. Wagoner's comment to me at the time was interesting. "Nobody wants to be the guy who runs General Motors when it goes out of business," he said. Was it possible that he already suspected the worst?

Wagoner didn't have many options. In many ways, GM wasn't being run just for its shareholders—and it hadn't been for forty years. Stakeholders such as workers and retirees (represented by the United Auto Workers) had as big an impact on corporate strategy as those who owned its stock. To some, GM looked more like a health care and pension provider than it did a car company.

Those obligations were crushing the company. In 2004, health care for GM's 1.1 million employees and retirees and their dependents had added $1,525 to the cost of every car and truck GM produced in North America. GM was buying more from Michigan Blue Cross than it did from any steel, glass, or rubber producer. Driven by giant increases in prescription-drug prices, GM's medical costs jumped 8.5 percent in 2004 and were expected to leap another 10.5 percent in 2005. GM was feeling the pain more than its competitors because after several decades of downsizing, it had two and a half retirees for every active worker. And the high costs were slamming profits. As 2005 got under way, GM was expecting to lay out $5.6 billion for medical care that year and was forecasting a profit in North America of just $500 million.

At the Detroit auto show in January 2005, Wagoner once again displayed his preference for incremental change. To deal with health care costs, he said, he was working to make medical-delivery systems more efficient and to get government help on catastrophic health care and malpractice reform. But he took two other options off the table. One was bankruptcy. When asked whether it was a possibility, Wagoner replied, "That's not a good idea. A lot of other things come along with Chapter 11, which basically end up in a lot of pain." That was one of the first times bankruptcy was discussed in connection with General Motors, but it wouldn't be the last.

The second option was to confront the United Auto Workers.

The UAW's membership had a better health care plan than most CEOs; it was certainly more lavish than that of GM's white-collar workers. UAW members didn't pay a cent for their health insurance, nor did they pay any deductibles. When a UAW member visited a doctor, he or she made only a tiny copay. Was it any wonder that Detroit seemed to have a denser concentration of chiropractors, podiatrists, and psychologists than anywhere else in the Western world? Or that GM's nickname around Detroit was "Generous Motors"?

Yet Wagoner refused to take on the union by publicly requesting it to reopen its contract. That was mostly because the union would dig in its heels when bargaining issues turned up in the press. "The minute you go public, the union shuts down," said an industry executive. "That doesn't work. But I think they [the UAW] are acutely aware they have a very rich benefit." Wagoner decided instead to play the inside game, negotiating with the union in private until he got a deal that would limit the impact of health care obligations on GM's balance sheet. It would produce one of his greatest achievements, but in the end it wouldn't be enough to stave off bankruptcy.

And so GM trundled on, trying to achieve the not entirely compatible objectives of making money for its shareholders at the same time that it paid its retirees' pension and health care bills. Yet some people still thought GM could pull itself out of trouble, and one of them was willing to put a considerable chunk of his personal fortune behind that belief: Kirk Kerkorian. The Las Vegas investor had been absent from the auto scene since his abortive run at Chrysler. But by the middle of 1996, Kerkorian had gathered up 9.9 percent of GM's stock. According to a spokesman, he saw "a company with very strong assets, a global reach, a historic cash flow that is very strong, and a lot of cash on hand that can be used to solve problems."

Kerkorian hadn't given an on-the-record interview in years, and even current pictures of him were scarce, so I didn't expend much energy in trying to track him down. His adviser, Jerry York, was another story. York was a former chief financial officer of Chrysler and seemed to love being an industry insider as much as he did the prospect of making money by driving up the stock price. He publicly commented on the deal just often enough to keep Wagoner and GM off balance.

At the end of June 2006, York, who had been named to GM's board of directors, launched a surprising initiative. He suggested that Renault, which had scored a big success turning around Nissan, acquire a 20 percent stake in GM and try to repeat the trick. Carlos Ghosn, who was CEO of both companies, was the reigning industry hero, and he was as attracted to the challenge of rescuing GM as York and Kerkorian were to the potential profits. According to a confidential analysis that I obtained later, the tie-up might have produced as much as $10 billion in operating profits per year for GM by 2011. That was a pretty compelling number for a company that had rung up $18.7 billion in losses in just the first six months of that year even then and needed to borrow $10 billion to $15 billion just to stay in business until 2010.

To be sure, the savings from a Renault alliance might have come at a steep price for GM's senior management. One proposed strategy called for a "repopulation" of GM's executive ranks with outside talent. That presumably would have forced some incumbent managers out of their jobs—a shocking development at a company where executives seem to enjoy lifetime employment. Exactly what would happen to Wagoner with Ghosn on the premises, or how the two would coexist, was left unclear.

Unenthusiastic though he may have been, Wagoner had little choice but to agree to talks with Ghosn. As expected, they went nowhere, and after several months the deal was scuttled. GM demanded cash compensation for what it said was the unequal division of synergies from a tie-up; Renault-Nissan refused to make any payments, saying they would be incompatible with the spirit of the alliance. That was fine with Wagoner, who argued that a tie-up with Renault "would have potentially been a distraction to our current turnaround efforts . . . and it could impede our fast-moving efforts to evolve a global management team."

Measured by the progress GM made since, the alliance might have been a good thing. But the two key personalities were clearly incompatible: Wagoner, the relaxed reformer, and Ghosn, the icy, numbers-driven turnaround king. With any opportunity for a quick score seemingly gone, Kerkorian decided to bail out. By the end of November 2006, he had sold substantially all of his remaining GM shares, and York left the GM board. Kerkorian had bought at the wrong time, but he was smart to sell when he did, disposing of some of his shares for thirty-three dollars. Three years later, GM stock was worthless.

Kerkorian was far from my thoughts as I tried to leverage what I thought might be an improving relationship with Wagoner into greater access at GM that would enable me to report on how he was actually running the company. Business writers are always on the outside looking in because the auto industry, because of its competitive pressures, is more closed to outsiders than most sectors of the economy. I fantasized about the drama and excitement taking place behind closed doors, and I wanted to see it firsthand. Besides, fly-on-the-wall reporting is one of the best ways to tell readers a story.

GM thought it had good news to report early in 2006, so the public relations staff allowed me to observe Wagoner in three situations that were typically closed to the press: meetings with dealers, with employees, and, in the holy grail of automotive journalism, with engineers in a product development meeting. I didn't uncover any revelations, but the situations would allow me to introduce far more color into a story than was normally available and add personal details to my portrayal of Wagoner.

So at seven o'clock on a Friday morning, I accompanied the CEO to a product meeting at GM's Design Center. As Wagoner reviewed the images of cars and trucks in development projected onto floor-to-ceiling video screens, he drove home his message that GM had to get faster, smarter, sharper. He was less successful creating a sense of urgency with some fifty dealers from the Washington, D.C., area, gathered in a suburban Virginia hotel conference room. "This is war," he told them. "The battle lines are being drawn tighter and tighter, and we need to push out." But the overall atmosphere said "patience' and "persistence" instead.

I came away more impressed by Wagoner than ever before—won over by his competitiveness and determination to do the right thing. Far from appearing beaten down by the company's problems, he seemed energized by them. "There's nothing like a good battle to raise the adrenaline and get everyone focused," he told me. Asked if he had second thoughts about casting his lot with the automaker instead of a high-paying job with a bank or consulting firm—he had never worked anywhere besides GM—he replied:

"If you are in it for the challenge, where else would you want to be than GM? I think it's the biggest game in town."

Even the best-trained executives are capable of less than prime-time moments: impatience, arrogance, irritation. But if Wagoner got tired of seeing me hanging around asking questions, he never was anything less than agreeable and responsive. From his reasoned, thoughtful answers, I concluded that he really knew what he was doing. Wagoner was no forty-thousand-foot manager; he was intimately involved in the key areas of the business. He was comfortable mixing it up with everyone from engineers to dealers. And he wasn't making any rash decisions.

Wagoner's patience, though, didn't sit well with everybody. "Rick Wagoner has made it clear that he will steer GM through this crisis with a strategy of gradual transition to a 'new' GM," stated Peter DeLorenzo, a former ad executive who writes the popular Detroit blog Autoextremist. "I contend that all they're really doing at this point is managing the continued downward spiral of the company while refusing to take the tough actions and make the hard choices needed." DeLorenzo would be proven right. It would take pressure from the White House and the bankruptcy court before GM developed a workable business plan.

As the auto beat reporter, I clearly was too close to Wagoner or GM to think the unthinkable, but another *Fortune* writer wasn't. Carol Loomis had worked at the magazine since 1954 and had long ago established a reputation as one of the best financial reporters in the business. She combined a willingness to crunch numbers with a delight in challenging the status quo that had led her to an unusual number of scoops over the preceding five decades. Only enhancing her reputation was her early journalistic discovery of Warren Buffett and her subsequent close friendship with him that included bridge games and editing his yearly message in the Berkshire Hathaway annual report.

Loomis was asked to look into GM's financial health, and she seized on the project with her usual energy and thoroughness. What resulted was a story in the February 20, 2006, issue that was dramatically splashed on the cover with white type against a black background and continued on for many pages inside. "It is the instinctive wish of most American businesspeople . . . that General Motors not go bankrupt," the story began. "And the evidence points, with increasing certitude, to bankruptcy."

The evidence she cited was not unique, but the way she arrayed it and the conclusions she was led to, backed by her blue-chip reputation, made for a compelling narrative. With its market share falling, GM was being starved of revenue, and its North American operation was burning cash. If gas went to three dollars a gallon or sales dropped by 5 percent or the economy went into recession, GM could be pushed to the wall, Loomis suggested. When all three happened in 2008, her dire prediction came true. Her prescience was uncanny.

With *Fortune* having declared that GM was on the verge of bankruptcy, I stood back for a year and a half. The story Loomis had written was an impossible act to follow: I would look foolish to contradict her with a positive story, whereas another negative piece would look like piling on. But I continued to watch and kept my lines to GM open in case an opportunity presented itself.

Labor costs were continuing to sap the company's strength. Long unsustainable, the UAW's lavish health and pension benefits for active and retired workers were threatening to bring down GM all on their own. By one calculation, each active worker was costing GM seventy-four dollars an hour once the benefits of retired workers were piled on. By comparison, Toyota's hourly wages and benefits at its American plants amounted to just forty-four dollars per hour because it had very few retirees. Besides the sheer dollars involved, GM's union contract made it grievously uncompetitive in cost—at a time when its products were substandard in other ways as well.

In public, the UAW insisted it would never reopen its contract to make concessions. In private, however, it began discussions with the company to see how it could help keep GM afloat. It had performed its own independent financial analysis of GM to better understand its financial condition, but it could have found out what it needed to know just by reading the newspaper: GM was heading toward insolvency.

In 2007, Wagoner won a historic agreement with the UAW to take retiree health care off the books and institute two-tier wages, and it seemed like time for another story. The bankruptcy of parts maker Delphi, which was still connected to GM, seemed to be nearing resolution. Recent GM models had won modest acceptance in the marketplace, suggesting that revenue and market-share problems might become a thing of the past. And the real-estate fueled economy was still perking along.

In meetings with investors, GM had been predicting a turnaround in 2010. Costs would be coming down; it expected to save between four billion and five billion dollars as a result of the union contract, and another five hundred million dollars as it untangled itself from Delphi. On the revenue side, GM expected industry sales to reach 16 million units in 2008 and 17 million a short while after that, driven by pent-up demand and a growing population. The demographic bulge of new drivers combined with a revised union contract could create a meaningful swing in earnings.

Here, I thought, was my chance to call a historic change before anybody else. So I plunged in with a big story in the January 21, 2008, issue headlined "Gentlemen, Start Your Turnaround." Despite recessionary storm clouds on the horizon, the congenital optimists at GM were more than happy to cooperate. "If you look generally at the key functions of the business," Wagoner told me, "I think we're running pretty well to very well in almost all of them." He noted, not for the last time, that the latest GM models, such as the Cadillac CTS and Chevy Malibu, were winning accolades. Adding my own two cents, I wrote, "If the determined, patient Wagoner can succeed in rescuing GM's homeland operations and return the automaker to consistent profitability, it would be a feat of historic proportions."

As it turned, he couldn't, and it wasn't. I had swallowed the GM Kool-Aid for the last time, and a spike in oil prices followed by a financial collapse and a brutal recession were about to crush Wagoner's hopes.

CHAPTER 18

The End of the Road

After my article appeared on January 8, 2008, suggesting that a real turnaround was at hand at GM, I got burned again. Just as in 1994, the publication of a story with a strong positive slant was followed by a string of negative events more calamitous than I could have imagined. GM was caught off guard by the run-up in oil prices as its truck sales cratered, destroying any hope of profits in North America. Despite hopeful pronouncements, Delphi, its former parts division and still financially dependent on GM, took another turn for the worse and sank deeper into bankruptcy. Meanwhile, the credit crunch was squeezing GMAC, GM's 49 percent-owned finance arm, leaving it unable to provide loans or leases to armies of potential customers. The macroeconomic forces—high oil prices followed by the credit crunch, bank failures, and recession—were no fault of GM's, but because it was already heavily leveraged, the company was stranded without a backup plan.

As it turned out, GM was in much worse financial shape than it appeared from the outside. The CTS and Malibu, always cited as examples of GM's growing prowess at product development, weren't even tips of the iceberg; the older cars that constituted most of the company's product lineup required massive marketing incentives to keep them from dying on dealers' lots. On February 12, 2008, GM reported a loss of $38.7 billion for all of 2007—an astounding number. The same day, it offered buyouts or early retirement to all seventy-four thousand of its U.S. hourly workers in order to hire lower-cost replacements. That was enough for me, and I threw in the towel. I had finally lost faith in GM, its optimistic projections for industry sales, its own expectations for a brighter future, and, sadly, Wagoner. It was finally clear to me that he had been too much of a gradualist and had been acting too slowly. The team of GM veterans he had left in place had failed him. Outside intervention now seemed essential to the company's survival.

Wagoner took a first step in that direction on March 3, when he named CFO Fritz Henderson president. Though yet another finance executive and a GM lifer, Henderson, forty-nine, seemed to be an excellent choice. Smart, confident, and quick off the mark, he had run GM operations on three continents. Henderson had been pointed out to me a decade earlier as GM's likely next leader, and his career never faltered. Though technically an insider, he had the perspective of an outsider, since he had worked only briefly in North America. Not everything he touched was successful—GM Europe refused to deliver consistent profits after his stint there—but Henderson avoided being tagged with any failures.

Henderson played the loyal lieutenant at a meeting with analysts and journalists in the walk-up to GM's annual meeting in June 2008, promising to align production and inventories more closely with demand, reduce structural costs, and produce more profit per car—all planks from Wagoner's platform. Meanwhile, the CEO was moving hesitantly to deal with GM's fatal mismatch with the market as the price of gasoline headed ever higher. In June, he announced GM would be closing four truck plants, though some wouldn't be shuttered until 2010. Even more belatedly, he declared that GM would begin a "strategic review" of its Hummer brand. Already the subject of jokes by late-night comedians because it epitomized the gas-hungry SUVs now falling from favor, Hummer had been out of sync with the American psyche for a year or two. By waiting so long to put it up for sale, Wagoner had all but destroyed its value to a potential buyer.

Finally, Wagoner began talking up a new small car, the Chevy Cruze, that GM would introduce in 2010 to replace the Chevy Cobalt. Those with long memories might have recalled that the Cobalt was also ballyhooed as a sensational new car when it replaced the Chevy Cavalier in 2004. But his claims were unconvincing because GM had a long history of overpromising and underdelivering. *Consumer Reports* had just surveyed twenty compact sedans from all manufacturers and had ranked the Cobalt seventeenth, not exactly a vote of confidence. The tradition of Corvair, Vega, and Chevette continued to weigh heavily.

Not that there was much Wagoner or Henderson could do to arrest the market's decline. In May 2008, GM sold only 268,892 vehicles in the United States, leaving it just a smidgen ahead of Toyota, which sold 257,404. With the trade-in value of light trucks and SUVs plummeting, GM was forced to take huge write-offs on vehicles returning from lease. Repeat customers were being kept out of the market because they didn't have enough equity in their old trucks to trade them in for new ones. The long-term consequences of the downturn were even scarier because GM was falling increasingly behind the competition. Writing for *Fortune*'s web site, CNN/Money.com, I observed: "Every time that gasoline prices have spiked, GM has gotten burned, and its Japanese competitors have out-maneuvered it at every turn: first into small cars, then to crossover vehicles, and now with hybrids and other fuel-saving technologies." Investors sold off GM stock, pushing its market capitalization below $8.5 billion (a mere $1 billion more than Cerberus had invested in Chrysler a year earlier).

I ratcheted up my criticism of Wagoner in the middle of July, when he announced another set of measures to deal with the gathering economic storm. The actions seemed modest to me and were accompanied by economic assumptions that he termed "conservative" but I deemed insufficient to cope with the crisis. One notable supposition was market share. Even though he was taking out one million units of truck capacity, he expected GM's market share to level off at 21 percent. Since GM's market share had been falling for more than thirty years, this seemed like a bad bet.

Still, unlike publications such as the *Wall Street Journal*, I wasn't calling for Wagoner's resignation just yet. I continued to believe that his combination of institutional knowledge and organizational support made him essential to any turnaround. But Wagoner couldn't catch a break. Just as the spike in oil prices eased in the fall, Lehman Brothers went bust, and the United States and the rest of the world were gripped by the credit crisis. Business everywhere came to a halt. In October, news broke that GM was talking to Chrysler about a merger, surely, I thought, a sign of desperation. Under the best of circumstances, auto company tie-ups are frightfully complicated because they require the integration of complex operations and product lines. The long model cycles in

the industry—eight years in most cases—make savings difficult to
capture quickly because so much time is needed. Pushing together
two failing companies like GM and Chrysler would be like tying
two boat anchors together: the resulting company would have excess capacity in people, products, plants, and dealers that it couldn't
afford.

GM strategists had a different view, and it turned out that they
had been flirting with Chrysler for more than a year. They envisioned absorbing Chrysler the way Chrysler had absorbed American Motors twenty years earlier, keeping the good parts and quickly
disposing of excess products and people. They saw promise in the
Jeep brand and wanted to merge the Dodge Ram pickup with similar models from Chevy and GMC to achieve economies of scale.
But Washington took a dim view of the deal because of the jobs
that would be lost at both companies, so the merger never went
forward. Chrysler would then turn to Italy's Fiat to save it.

With its alternatives exhausted, there seemed to be little left for
GM to do but to look for government help. On November 18,
2008, Wagoner, along with the CEOs of Ford and Chrysler and
UAW president Ron Gettelfinger, appeared at a four-and-a-half-
hour hearing in the House Financial Services Committee to make
an application for a government "bridge loan." They might as well
have stayed home. The CEOs' decision to travel on their individual corporate jets got them off to a bad start from which they never
recovered. Once again, Detroit looked clueless and out of touch.

For his part, Wagoner seemed unprepared for his congressional appearance. This was his chance to explain why GM and Detroit were important to America. Instead, he delivered the same
ritualized presentation he might have given to a group of stock-

holders, talking up the company's bright prospects. As one joker
put it, if the American Cancer Society asked for funds the way GM
did, there'd be no hope for a cure. Like Fred Donner and Jim
Roche before him, Wagoner was tone deaf when appearing on a
national stage. He had to tread a narrow line between showing that
he was doing everything he could to save the company at the same
time that he was asking for help, and he couldn't pull it off. He
didn't bother to acknowledge that GM had lost an astounding
seventy-two billion dollars in the past four years on his watch, including fifty-one billion dollars before the crisis hit in 2008. Instead, with a straight face, he blamed GM's problems not on its
products, its business plans, or its long-term strategy but on the
"global financial crisis."

Even on an open court, Wagoner couldn't sink a layup. When
asked if he would accept a dollar-a-year salary as part of the bailout,
the way Lee Iacocca did to get government loan guarantees for
Chrysler, Wagoner botched a great opportunity. Instead of grandly
offering to sacrifice his pay if it would save the company, Wagoner
replied churlishly that he had already taken a 50 percent salary cut
earlier and lost most of the value of thousands of shares of GM
stock he had purchased over the years. He went downhill from
there. When the question arose whether GM would accept, as a
condition of the loan, even tougher fuel economy rules, Wagoner
complained, "We are stretching to meet the requirements as they
are." And when asked if he would pledge not to come back for
more help if he got aid this time, Wagoner said he would "if you'll
make a pledge that the economy will turn around by a certain
date." That may have been the correct answer, but it wasn't the
right one.

After two days of questions from Congress, Wagoner appeared on the *NewsHour with Jim Lehrer,* where he was interviewed by Judy Woodruff. He was asked what had become the question of the moment—why GM and the rest of Detroit didn't make the kind of cars that the American people need and want. It is actually an interesting question for GM, because the world's largest automaker seemed particularly inept at making passenger cars and hadn't produced a bona fide hit in years. The best Wagoner could come up with was the lukewarm claim that "generally our products are considered to be quite successful." He mentioned for what seemed like the thousandth time his two favorites: the Chevy Malibu and Cadillac CTS—hardly a ringing endorsement for the rest of GM's product line—and then acknowledged that there had been mistakes in the past. "So, hey, maybe there's some history there. You know, for that, I can't change it."

Wagoner's moment in the public spotlight was coming to an end, but the pain didn't stop. For the first eleven months of 2008, GM's sales fell 21.9 percent. On December 4, Wagoner was back in Washington, testifying before the Senate about GM's future business plans. This time, he made his arrival in an electric Chevrolet Volt prototype, an odd choice for a company in distress, since the Volt was about as relevant to GM's economic survival as an electric pogo stick. By the time it goes into production in late 2010, GM will have invested a billion dollars in the Volt's development without any prospect of a profit. The car will be expensive, and its volumes will be small.

During this second Washington session, there was no more brave talk about making better cars, more economical cars, or more alternative-fuel cars. Wagoner said that GM would be out of business unless it got an immediate four-billion-dollar loan and that the company would need more after that to get it through the crisis. But aside from some window-dressing items such as reducing executive compensation and selling corporate airplanes, he didn't say much about new ways of doing business. He should have. GM had been cutting costs since the 1980s. But it never became more profitable because its revenue shrank faster than its costs.

On December 19, 2008, the government money arrived in the form of $13.4 billion in emergency loans, part of the $700 billion Troubled Asset Relief Program. Still, GM's future was becoming increasingly precarious. On February 17, 2009, the company requested an additional $16.6 billion in government loans and said it would run out of cash as soon as March without new federal funding. Wagoner would not be around to see its request approved. On March 29, his eight-and-a-half-year run as CEO came to an ignominious end. When he arrived at the Treasury Department for a meeting with the auto task force, Wagoner was a thirty-two-year GM veteran and a chief executive carrying the weight of the company's wrenching restructuring on his six-foot, four-inch frame. But when Treasury rejected GM's second request for more funding, the White House pushed him out; auto task force leader Steven Rattner asked for Wagoner's resignation. Henderson was named CEO, while board member Kent Kresa became interim chairman. Wagoner, it was reported later, never saw it coming. Those who glimpsed him later that day returning to Detroit on a commercial flight noted the dejected slump in his shoulders. "In the course of that meeting, they requested that I step aside as CEO of GM, and so I have," Wagoner said in a message posted on the automaker's web site, a good company man to the end.

Wagoner deserved better. As I wrote for Fortune.com on the day that Wagoner's ouster became public: "If Wagoner had retired on January 1, 2008, instead of March 29, 2009, he might have been remembered as one of GM's greatest leaders. Without fanfare, he negotiated an historic agreement with the United Auto Workers to reduce the burden of pension and health care costs and to make its hourly labor costs more competitive. He was also in the final stages of the consolidation of GM's North American operations after a century of balkanization. At last, what was then the world's largest auto company would be able to leverage its global scale to become cost- and efficiency-competitive."

But he lost his chance when the economy collapsed, and he failed to react quickly enough in the crisis. "This is not meant as a condemnation of Mr. Wagoner, who has devoted his life to this company," President Obama said a few days later in laying out a restructuring strategy for GM. "It's a recognition that it will take a new vision and new direction to create the GM of the future."

Wagoner had done himself no favors by publicly refusing to consider bankruptcy as an option. His continual insistence that GM would be irretrievably damaged because of a lack of confidence in the company and its brands rang hollow in the absence of compelling evidence. Rightly or wrongly, Wagoner was seen as an oblivious defender of the status quo. Yale School of Management professor Jeffrey Sonnenfeld was especially harsh, accusing him of being "a product of GM's dangerous cultural mindset" who drove the company "back into past calamitous potholes." For Sonnenfeld, Wagoner was a worse CEO than Roger Smith because rather than learn from Smith's mistakes, Wagoner repeated them. He was especially critical of his performance in Washington. "Wagoner continally went before the American people and Congress unprepared and angry, demanding taxpayer support without ever being able to articulate why he wanted $25 billion, how the company would use the money, and what GM's vision was for a future viable enterprise."

Henderson was more of a realist than Wagoner and could read the handwriting on the wall. He repeatedly signaled that he found bankruptcy acceptable. That made him look smart. In the end, a court-ordered reorganization with the strong backing of the federal government turned out to be the best mechanism for getting GM in fighting shape. On June 1, 2009, once-mighty General Motors followed Chrysler into bankruptcy. It would emerge forty-four days later as a new company with four fewer brands, as well as fewer executives, employees, dealers, and debt. The old GM—the company that had been a colossus—was dead. What the future held for the new one was to be determined.

Epilogue

In the summer and early fall of 2009, I spent time with GM's new CEO, Fritz Henderson. In addition to a pair of formal interviews, we did some driving together at GM's proving ground in Milford, Michigan. We never got lost in the countryside as I had with Rick Wagoner years earlier, but I did sit in the passenger seat while Henderson took a Cadillac CTS through a handling course consisting of plastic cones lined up on a paved surface. Demonstrating my inability to learn from experience, I kept Henderson talking the whole time, which kept him from fully demonstrating his driving skills—or me from observing them. An accountant by training, he carefully made sure he left all the cones standing by negotiating the course at snail-like speed.

At first glance, Henderson resembles Wagoner in overdrive. They have had similar careers: both graduated from Harvard Business School and went on to GM's treasurer's office in New York, and both ran GM operations in Brazil. But Henderson does more than talk faster and act more quickly. Over the course of our conversations and interviews, he made it clear that he is less beholden to GM's old ways and more demanding of results. When the government's auto task force insisted on a more rigorous revitalization plan, it was Henderson who made the tough calls to discontinue Pontiac and put Saturn up for sale. And Henderson presciently saw bankruptcy as a smart option for GM and developed a plan to restructure the company.

Henderson has also made it clear that he understands the new world order at GM. He is working for a board of directors he didn't select, headed by a chairman who represents GM's largest shareholder, the U.S. government. Whereas the old board cut Wagoner an enormous amount of slack, Henderson readily admits to being on a short leash and claims to be okay with that. Nor is he working at an industry leader any more. Once a towering presence, GM is now an underdog, given a second chance at life only because of bankruptcy. Henderson is quick to note that there will be no third chance. Whether his executive team is equally attuned to the new realities is another question. Like Henderson, all but Lutz are GM lifers who have spent as long as four decades with the company. They give lip service to the idea that their outlook will be different this time. But once in a while their facade slips and there are glimpses of the old, arrogant, insular GM.

Indeed, GM's new managers are part of a culture at GM that has resolutely resisted new ideas over the years, whether they came from competitors like Toyota or internally from the Saturn experiment. And the chances of a flurry of new concepts now finding their way into Henderson's GM don't seem any better. GM has been unsuccessful in attracting any outsiders to the company who might provide some fresh thinking. Asked why, with the plethora of automotive talent available in the economic downturn, none have been recruited by GM, Henderson blames government pay ceilings and the lack of first-rate talent. Whatever the reason, fresh air is needed at GM, and it isn't getting as much as it needs.

In the early going, the Henderson administration seemed as left-footed as any GM team since Roger Smith's. A much-publicized experiment to sell cars on eBay was abruptly canceled, and a post-bankruptcy ad campaign starring board chairman Ed Whitacre got poor reviews. More substantively, a deal to sell Saturn to entre-preneur Roger Penske collapsed, and the new board of directors reversed Henderson's plan to sell part of Opel to parts maker Magna. To be sure, GM's new Chevrolets and Cadillacs were get-ting a better reception from reviewers and in the marketplace, but so were other makers' cars. Solid evidence to show that the new GM was performing better than the old one was hard to come by, and Henderson's leash seemed as short as ever. When he finally resigned in December after less than nine months on the job, his decision was anticlimactic.

In the end, whether GM survives depends in large part on the health of the American car market. If car sales pick up, GM could earn its fair share and make a nice profit. Under its new, postbank-ruptcy structure, it is designed to break even with industry sales at ten million cars and trucks a year. That's a huge improvement over the old GM, which required industry sales of sixteen million units before it turned a profit. But if U.S. sales remain below ten million, as they did in 2009, GM's prospects are significantly dimmed.

For GM to thrive requires a higher level of achievement. It has to develop cars and trucks that are not just as good as but better than the competition and that begin to appeal not just to red state customers but to more critical buyers on the coasts. Then it has to convince customers to purchase these cars through smarter marketing that makes a Buick as appealing as an Audi or a Chevy Cruze hotter than a Honda Civic. And it has to be a leader in technology that is important enough to consumers for them to pay a premium for it. GM is demonstrating some progress in all those areas, but success is a long way off.

Over at Ford, CEO Alan Mulally was looking smarter and smarter as 2009 ended, hailed by some as the best industry leader since GM's Sloan. Ford sales were picking up, and the company got a boost in public esteem from its decision not to take government aid. But even Mulally would have to admit that the praise was premature. Ford was launching two core models in 2010, the Fiesta and the Focus, whose success was vital to the company but whose prospects were uncertain. They had been developed in Europe to higher specifications—and higher prices—than Americans were used to paying for their small cars. If gasoline costs kept rising, they could become big successes; if prices stayed low, the cars would find less enthusiasm in the marketplace.

The United Auto Workers, which used to have a cozy relationship with Ford, was also causing some headaches for Mulally. As usual, the union rank-and-file seemed to focus on obtaining the highest level of wages and benefits for themselves without regard for the health of the companies that paid those wages and benefits or their ability to employ union workers in the future. In October 2009, they were rebelling against a new contract that would have placed them on the same financial footing as their union brothers and sisters at GM and Chrysler, who had made concessions in order to help those companies emerge from bankruptcy. Although the new contract wasn't a make-or-break for Ford's future, its rejection would keep the company's costs high and shrink potential profits. As for the union, its actions made the UAW look short-sighted and greedy once again.

Still, there was no doubt that Ford, having escaped bankruptcy and government intervention in its management, was positioned more solidly than either of its Detroit competitors. It had gained nearly a point of market share during the first nine months of 2009, and several of its car lines were winning accolades. Perhaps Ford's biggest worry was how long Mulally would remain on the job. Ford's history of bumpy leadership transitions would rival that of some Latin American countries, and there was no clear-cut succes-sor to Mulally in place to prevent another palace upheaval.

At Chrysler, meanwhile, the automotive world was waiting to see what magic CEO Sergio Marchionne would be able to per-form. He was attacking Chrysler's two biggest weaknesses—lack of a long-term product plan, and lack of a short-term product plan—and announced his intention to put a new emphasis on marketing and brands. Some of his ideas sounded familiar, but others were fresh and seemed promising. Marchionne got lower marks, how-ever, for his prediction that Chrysler would double its sales in the next five years.

As filled with question marks as Marchionne's long-term plan might be, at least it had the advantage of containing actual new models. For 2010 and 2011, Chrysler has almost nothing new to offer customers. That will hurt Chrysler's market share, which has fallen below 10 percent, and force it to continue its destructive prac-tice of selling nearly half its production to rental car fleets. Without an unexpected boom in car sales, Chrysler's chances of surviving seem uncertain. Its previous owners have left the pipeline dry of attractive and saleable product, and Marchionne simply doesn't have enough time to fill it.

The events of 2009 were not a happy ending for the country that popularized the automobile, made it an important part of its culture, and dominated the global industry for nearly a century. But even in this mature, capital-intensive industry, nothing remains constant. The auto business is too dynamic to be controlled within any one country's borders and more open to change than anyone has expected. For years, experts have been predicting that the industry would consolidate into four or five global super-groups, under the assumption that economies of scale are essential to survival and that the vast sums needed to engineer and market cars will provide barriers to entry by new competitors. Instead, the industry has fractured. Boutique manufacturers have sprung up in California, and new mass-market automakers have emerged in Korea, China, and India. Instead of being a closed shop, making cars has become a free-for-all.

As for the collapse of Detroit and the voyage of two of its players through bankruptcy in 2009, it resembles nothing so much as the failure of the British auto industry two generations earlier. Companies caught up in their own traditions and unwilling to change, preyed upon by hungry labor unions with their own interests at heart, couldn't keep up with the competition and collapsed under their own weight. There is no longer a locally owned auto industry in Great Britain. All of its best-known brands—Jaguar, Land Rover, Bentley, Rolls-Royce, Aston Martin, Vauxhall—today are owned by non-British companies.

The most important lesson learned from the events of 2009 is that the United States needs a domestic auto industry for its jobs, technology, wealth creation, trading balances, and prestige. But it isn't entitled to one—every day it needs to earn the right to keep one. Americans should hope that Ford's recovery and GM's and Chrysler's emergence from bankruptcy have provided the horse-power to push the needle on the industry's speedometer back up the dial. If it hasn't, they should be prepared to see Detroit go the way of Great Britain.

Index

Index

Index

loans, 229; board of directors, 163, 164; Chevrolet spies at, 47; cost cutting measures, 184; decision-making strategy, 73; departures of chief executives, 9, 183; design and styling, 26, 162; economic recession and, 159; European sales and modifications, 160–61; federal investigation of, 182; financial difficulties, 183, 185; firings at, 71–72, 73, 77, 78, 79–80; "Ford 2000" project, 161–62, 166, 167; future product programs, 180; global unification plan, 160, 161, 187–88; history, 9, 80, 179, 185, 189, 191, 239; hourly employees, 185; management, 74, 75, 76, 78, 180; nonfamily executives, 72, 79, 80; North American operations, 160; office politics and intrigues, 6, 71, 72, 179, 180, 239; operating margins, 63; price of cars, 15; production costs, 63; product-led recovery, 76; profits, 134, 162, 166; quality problems, 182–83; recovery, 241; refusal of federal aid, 9, 137, 186–87, 189, 238; reorganization plan, 9, 156, 161, 211; return of stock to shareholders, 155; revenue per vehicle, 155; salaried employees, 161, 185; sales, 167, 174, 182, 183; shares, 71, 74; stock, 155, 185; succession issues at, 159, 163–66; UAW and, 142, 238

Ford, Bill Jr., 74, 75–76, 162, 163, 164, 166, 167; as CEO, 179–80, 183, 185; customer relations, 181; Edsel Ford and, 181; environmental views of, 179, 180; Nasser and, 182–83, 184; personality, 179–81; revitalization plan, 184

Ford, Edsel, 74–76, 76, 77, 162–63, 164, 181

Ford, Edsel II, 74

Ford, Henry, 33, 62, 71, 72

Ford, Henry II, 72–73, 94–95, 162, 185

Ford, Josephine, 74

Ford, William Clay, 74

Ford family, 9, 71, 72, 74, 76, 77, 80, 159, 183; battles with executives, 160; competition within, 163; dissident members of, 184; financial difficulties, 184–85

Ford models: Contour, 161; Country Squire station wagon, 25; Edsel, 34; Escort, 160; Explorer, 128, 161, 166, 181–82; F150, 161; Fiesta, 188, 238; Focus, 162, 188, 238; LTD, 45; Mercury, 124; minivans, 9; Model T, 33, 62; Mondeo, 160–61; Mustang, 82, 201, 203; Ranch Wagon, 26; Ranger, 128, 181–82; Sable, 79, 161; SUVs, 161; Taurus, 76, 79, 108, 161; trucks, 9, 161, 166

foreign exchange rates, 176

Fortune 500, 177

Fortune magazine, 32, 54, 56, 66, 220; advertising in, 9; article on Bill Ford, 180–81, 184; article on Buick, 109–10; article on Eaton at Chrysler, 134; article on Ford, 72, 163–64, 187–88; article on Ford's six-billion-dollar-car, 161; article on GM turnaround, 130–31, 145; article on Jack Smith, 130–31, 132; article on Ross Perot, 68; article on the Ford family, 74, 75; articles on GM, 10; articles on GM's impending demise, 107–8, 112–13; articles on Iacocca, 94, 98, 201, 202, 203, 208; articles on production at GM, 146–47; articles on Steve Jobs, 93; articles on the impending demise of GM, 113, 121, 153; automobile cover, 59; automotive journalism at, 6, 8; on departure of Wagoner from GM, 156–57; interview with Peterson at Ford, 73, 75, 79; interview with Roger Smith, 64

Index

France, 4

Free Press (Detroit), 31–32, 40, 54, 55, 72, 95–96

fuel economy/efficiency, 99, 144, 169, 230

gas prices, 86, 170, 188, 221, 227, 238

General Motors Assembly Division (GMAD), 20, 60, 61

General Motors (general discussion): advertising, 151, 152, 237; auto loans, 213; battery-operated cars, 50–51; board of directors, 30, 114, 115, 211, 213, 217; bond rating, 212–13; brand affiliations, 123; brand descriptions, 122; brand managers and marketing, 126, 148–50, 151, 153, 172, 191; brand overlap, 44, 123; business model, 220; centralized operations, 172; committee structure, 37, 39, 40, 42, 43, 49, 65, 67, 75, 115, 119, 163; competitive shortcomings, 104, 106–7; corporate headquarters, 37–38, 41; corporate overhead, 108; cost of cars, 231; cost of manufacturing, 128, 198; cost of workforce, 111; costs, 97, 155, 213–14, 222; decision-making problems, 39, 41, 43; decision-making strategy, 67, 68; departures of chief executives, 9; Design Center, 219; divisions, 16, 17; downsizing efforts, 110, 112, 215; earnings, 14, 144, 155; employees, 52, 61, 119, 122, 146, 177, 215; environmentalists and, 50–51; financial difficulties, 83, 99, 108, 110, 119–20, 121, 147, 155–58, 177, 221, 230; financial policy, 38; firing of executives, 46, 85, 217–18; former employees, 8; globalization, 89, 172, 217, 218; health care obligations, 147, 176, 200, 214, 215, 233; hourly employees, 226; internal history, 1, 37, 58, 61, 65, 113, 156, 161, 170, 177, 191; internal problems, 109; international operations, 116; as largest automotive maker, 1, 2, 7–8, 11, 30, 32, 36, 43, 51, 105, 136–37, 231, 233; lawsuits and investigations of, 34–36, 49; loss of revenue, 212, 226, 230; management, 18, 39–40; manufacturing, 123, 125–26; manufacturing costs, 129; marketing, 63, 113, 122, 226; marketing strategies, 148, 151–52; monopoly in auto industry, 15–17; net earnings, 174; North American operations, 115, 120, 144, 147, 153, 155, 169, 171, 172, 178, 211–12, 214, 221, 233; operating margins, 63; organizational problems, 158; pension obligations, 66, 120, 147, 176, 200, 214, 215, 216–17, 233; post bankruptcy, 2, 235–36, 237, 241; price of cars, 15, 84, 157; product development, 42, 43, 108, 148, 158, 173, 195, 197, 198, 219, 225; production, 60, 111, 113, 125; production costs, 18, 63, 111, 113, 215; production failures, 146–47; production statistics, 15; product lines, 1, 231; product quality, 147; profit margin, 33, 155, 178, 226, 239; profits, 134, 214, 215; public image, 33, 49–50, 57; public relations, 19, 48, 57, 219; purchasing operations, 121, 123; rebellion by the board of directors, 105, 170; remaking of image, 8; reorganization plan, 154; reorganization plan under Roger Smith, 59–64, 69, 81, 84, 85; reputation, 21, 36–37, 51, 87, 200; restructuring of, 232, 233, 234; restructuring/reorganization, 20, 59–64, 81, 84, 85; revenues, 155, 157, 214; salaried employees, 40–41, 232; sales, 40, 63, 64, 86, 97, 105, 107, 109, 111–12, 117, 121, 132, 144–47, 151, 154, 170,

Index